BEWARE . . .

You are about to enter an ESCAPE BOOK. If you don't know what one of those is, then perhaps we should explain. An escape book is a form of puzzle book in which the unwary reader may become trapped for eternity. It is an escape room in the form of a book. You can decide on your own path, but your route is often controlled by the solutions you give to the puzzles you encounter along the way. You must solve the puzzles to escape the pages.

Some puzzles will offer you alternative routes according to your solution. Others will invite you to calculate the next entry you should turn to. When this happens, you should check the 'from' number at the top left to ensure that you came from the right location. If you find that you have arrived from the wrong place, you should turn back and think again.

Not all wrong solutions will end the story. As befits an adventure in which you play the role of Sherlock Holmes, this book is far more cunning than that. Some wrong answers may have unforeseen consequences further down the path, causing you to miss a helpful clue or even land a red herring.

While you are trapped inside the escape book, you should pay attention to everything you see. Once the game is afoot, there are all manner of clues hidden on the pages. Use Watson's Notebook – which you will discover shortly – to record your observations. Some of these notes might be needed to solve later puzzles. You will also be required to master the Code Wheel, located on the cover of the book (of which, more later). If you are struggling with your art of deduction, you will find some helpful hints and clues (and even the answers) located at 221A and 221B, found at the back of the book.

There is more than one door through which you can exit the Escape Book. Some doors are marked with triumph . . . others with infamy. Only the most observant of detectives will find an escape route that results in newspaper headlines proclaiming their heroic success.

> ▶ *These arrows direct you to your next entry.*
> *Now, all great adventures begin by turning the first page . . .*

WATSON'S NOTEBOOK

Use this notebook to jot down anything of interest you encounter during your adventure; you may find it helps you to solve a later puzzle.

NOTES & OBSERVATIONS

....

....

....

....

....

....

....

....

....

....

....

....

....

....

....

....

....

▶ *If you have yet to begin your adventure, turn over the page.*
(Feel free to refer to Watson's Notebook at any time.)

THE STORY

In the upcoming adventure, which takes place principally within the historic Tower of London complex, you will take on the role of the world's most famous consulting detective, Sherlock Holmes, as he becomes trapped within a dastardly plot. You will see everything from his point of view and attempt to solve the puzzles with his powers of deduction. You will be him! Try to think in the way that Sherlock thinks. As he once said, in Sir Arthur Conan Doyle's *The Sign of the Four* (1890): "When you have eliminated the impossible, whatever remains, HOWEVER IMPROBABLE, must be the truth."

You will be accompanied, of course, by your faithful companion Doctor John H. Watson. He will offer you words of advice, a voice of reason and a steady hand in times of peril. You should also make good use of his notebook to record observations that may help with your escape.

This adventure is set in 1896, five years after the fight between Holmes and his great rival Professor James Moriarty at the Reichenbach Falls in which both were thought to have died. But Holmes survived and returned. And he now has his suspicions that his rival is also back . . . seemingly from the dead.

Taking an autumn walk by the River Thames, Holmes and Watson notice a poster advertising a musical entertainment. As part of ceremonies celebrating Queen Victoria becoming Britain's longest-reigning monarch, a concert has been scheduled for the following day, 23 September 1896, by an outdoor orchestra on Tower Bridge in the presence of Her Majesty. Intriguingly the performance is of an orchestral suite, 'Sweet Thames Run Softly', composed by Odon von Mihalovic. Wasn't he the chap who had recently written to 221B with a rather far-fetched story about a plot?

While returning home, our heroes encounter a challenge painted on the pavement that catches their attention – and ends up leading them into an irresistible network of puzzles within the Tower of London, in which they quickly see the hand of an old and all-too-familiar adversary. And could there be a connection to the concert scheduled for the next morning on the Bridge? Is the queen in danger? Could Odon von Mihalovic be involved?

THE CODE WHEEL

Set into the cover of this escape book is a code wheel, which is an essential part of your equipment for solving some of the puzzles you will encounter. It features a series of windows behind which are letters, numbers, colours and a sequence of symbols. These can be used in a number of ways:

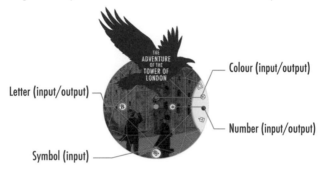

You can find a digital version of the Code Wheel at:
https://www.ammonitepress.com/gift/sherlock-tower-of-london-wheel/

In some puzzles you'll discover coded messages in the form of unintelligible notes or secret symbols hidden in the story. Using the code wheel, input your discoveries in the relevant *input* dial, then decode them by reading the relevant *ouput* dial.

To begin your adventure, you must first unlock the escape book. To do this, you should use the code wheel to solve the following cipher:

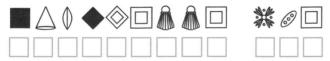

▶ *The answer will lead you into the story by describing something you are enjoying in entry 1. Once you have solved it, please put the code wheel away until the moment in the story when you receive the code wheel and are told to begin using it.*

"SWEET THAMES RUN SOFTLY"

"Buck up, Holmes, we'd better get a move on." Watson pulls you from your reverie. Early afternoon sunlight glints off the blue metal sections of Tower Bridge, reflecting onto the water and back to the bridge in an endless reverberation. Watson is still at your elbow. "What are they setting up over there?" he asks.

You gesture absent-mindedly to a poster. "A concert."

"Sweet Thames Run Softly," Watson reads aloud. "Performed live on the Bridge tomorrow morning. It's a piece by our old friend Odon von M . . ."

"Is it really?" you ask. "Do you recall he was bothering us a month or so back with some far-fetched story about a plot . . . Tedious, as I recall."

You are about to turn away, then stop in your tracks. The cobbles in front of you are covered in wet paint, still glinting.

Watson boggles at it. "A message, Holmes! Addressed to you."

You read it aloud:

> *Now Holmes, old chap, a surprise to see you here! Ultimately, we've got to decide which way to go. Might I suggest a look at the arrows? Bright eyes catch those who don't shift in the cross. Estaablish their position. Round it off by bringing them together.*

"I guess we're taking a little diversion on our way back to 221B," you say. You cast your eye around, and spot a number of street signs, each with a small arrow. They read: Cross Lane, St Dunstan's Hill, Lower Thames Street and Great Tower Street.

Watson has stepped closer to the drying paint. "There's a diagram here, next to 'cross'. Two dotted lines, one horizontal, one vertical," he says.

You're already puzzling your way through.

▶ *Turn to the passage you reveal.*

② LOOKING FOR A BOTTLE

"Your adversary is intolerable," huffs Watson. "He's telling us to be braver. How dare he?"

"And to look for a bottle, as well," you add. "His meaning is pretty clear, especially in concert with the riddle he left." Not for the first time tonight, your mind strays to the concert tomorrow morning. You wonder about Moriarty's plan.

Watson falls in with your search, and you begin to seek out a bottle in the area around the Coldharbour Tower ruins. No luck. The light is beginning to fade. Of course, since Watson knocked your watch into a glass of gin at the Yeoman Warders' Club you cannot tell the exact time. But given the time of year and the deepening shadows, your estimate would be 6:33 p.m.

"If it's not here, where we are, how the devil can we find a bottle in this vast enclosure and so many buildings?" asks Watson.

"We have managed many a task far harder in our career, Watson. Be calm." You are beginning to enjoy this.

You both spread out, eyes expertly scanning far and wide. Thank goodness your vision is so keen. Although only a few yards' distant, Watson seems mercifully far away. All at once you stop, hearing a sequence of notes.

"Be silent, Watson!"

"What? I said nothing!"

"Were you not whistling or singing?"

"No, Holmes, not a breath."

As before, when you heard music on Tower Green, the notes make you shiver. You pause. Watson is suddenly at your side, handing you something long, thin, cold – it's another Stradivarius string. You barely register it, simply taking it and pocketing it. You are caught up with the notes, the eerie reverie. As you search the shadows for their source you see a flurry of movement, a flick of reddish-gold hair?

"Did you see?"

Watson's eyes are in the sky, watching the ravens. Again, the notes sound.

▶ *To continue to look for the bottle, turn to 44.*

▶ *To follow the music, turn to 66.*

THE WINGS

"To the Broad Arrow Tower," you say, rolling up the map and tucking it into your pocket.

Watson continues to look stumped. You did move relatively quickly. Good to give him some time to catch up.

You take out the map and the note and take a moment to explain your methods.

"See here," you explain, pointing at the note. "This emboldened A is telling us to use the code wheel to find the letter A. The A is red in the code wheel, so are the wings, and we're headed to Broad Arrow Tower."

"What about these other emboldened letters, though?" Watson asks.

You look again, and discover he is indeed right. There are several emboldened words you missed.

Begrudgingly you return to the puzzle for another look.

► *Return to 88.*

EFGB

You play the notes EFGB. Nothing happens.

Nothing at all. You were sure that would be right. What can have gone wrong?

You try again. Time seems to stand still in the cage.

Behind you, Watson groans.

► *Turn to 57.*

THE JEWEL ROOM

"I make it five words," Watson says, "And on the map, 5 indicates . . . upstairs in this same tower."

You are on the stairs before him and enter the room on the top floor.

"This is the Jewel Room, built only 28 years ago," he says, "where the Crown Jewels are –"

He falls silent. In the centre of the room is a large fenced enclosure, without doubt to house the jewels in normal times. But it is quite empty.

"Where in God's name can they be?" Watson says. "Can Moriarty have stolen them as part of his wicked scheme?"

"I don't doubt they're involved, my dear fellow," you say, drawing a deep breath. "But the plot must be bigger than just a theft. Moriarty has boasted of a threat on Tower Bridge. What threat could the Crown Jewels being missing pose?"

Watson grunts. He plucks another note from the railings.

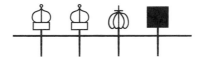

Dear Struggling Sherlock, Wandering Watson,
    I hope our tour of the Tower is giving you both pleasure.
I am sorry that you cannot enjoy seeing the Crown Jewels in all
their splendour. No doubt you are wondering whether I intend
to steal them. Nothing so obvious. I will soon, with the help of a
friend, have access to the great wealth of a famous ecclesiastical
institution . . .
    For now, look up to see. Take a step forward to decode and
turn around to find the way.

▶ *Decode the clues to find your next destination.*
  Look it up on the map and turn to that number.

⑥ DINNER IN THE SALT TOWER

Using the map you find your way to the next destination: the Salt Tower.

"Where is all this leading us, Holmes?" Watson grumbles.

"Patience. This is a delicious challenge. I've never been bettered by Moriarty yet." You are aware nevertheless that the professor can be up to no good . . . the note outside clearly implied you and Watson would be seen as traitors and there was the threat concerning the Bridge and the morning . . .

Meanwhile a close inspection of the ground floor yields no clues, so you climb upstairs into a pentagonal chamber with a huge stone fireplace.

"This place, by the way, was John Balliol Tower because no less a figure than he was jailed here." Watson rattles on. "Then it became the Salt Tower. Perhaps it was used for storing salt – as you know, a rare commodity and only available to those 'above the salt' on high table, so to speak."

You are on the prowl. On one wall you see an ancient piece of graffiti scratched in the plaster. At a glance you would estimate it was 350 to 400 years old. It reads: *Seek freedom beneath the water*.

"See this, old man?" asks Watson. "What on earth could that mean?"

How delightfully difficult. You lodge it in your memory and carry on looking.

Watson has taken a guidebook from his pocket and is reading: "Many celebrated figures were jailed here, including Princess Elizabeth's tutor Giovanni Castiglioni, Bristol innkeeper Hew Draper, Scottish ruler John Balliol, Jesuits John Gerard and Michael Moody – and perhaps their fellow Catholic John Arden . . . I say, what's this?" From the fireplace he lifts a twist of paper and opens it. White grains spill out. "What the devil? The very substance! Astounding . . . And a message."

Prisoners dining left to right around the table: Castiglioni has a single plate; Gerard, a plate, knife and fork; Arden, just one cup; Moody, a spoon, knife, fork and plate; Balliol, three plates and no cutlery; while Draper has the same as Balliol plus a knife and a cup. I count on you to spell it out. At this meal they address one another by their second names only.

"Clearly whoever wrote this note – one assumes Moriarty himself – has the same guidebook and interest in the history of the Tower as you, Watson. Curious."

Watson rubs his finger vigorously across his absurd moustache.

► *You can't work out the code. Turn to 87.*

► *Use the code to find a word – your next destination. Find it on the map and turn to that number.*

CONSTABLE TOWER

from 75

Following the clue, you arrive at the Constable Tower. As always, you inspect each new place very closely.

"What have we here, Watson?"

He looks absurdly pleased that you are asking for his explanation. "Well," he enthuses, "this was the home of the Constable of the Tower, the commanding officer appointed by the monarch."

There are no clues or apparent messages on the ground floor, so you take the winding stairs up. As you near the top there appears to be a movement in the air ahead of you – and do you hear footsteps receding? But you are unable to catch up with anyone and when you reach the top of this staircase you come into a comfortably appointed living room or office. There is plenty of evidence that someone has recently been here.

"Is someone helping us . . . or hindering?" You ponder aloud.

"If someone wants to help us, why would they not be more open about it?" Watson says, "There's no one about."

"It's surely rather obvious, old chum. There appears to be no one about but there's no knowing who is in the shadows. Whoever's helping us may need to stay hidden."

On the central table is a light meal of sandwiches and cake, with a decanter of some fine wine or other. On the floor beside two enticing easy chairs, is a recently disturbed pile of papers. Beyond is a desk. In one corner, a drinks cabinet. Watson sniffs.

"Where is everyone? I wonder how Moriarty got everyone to leave."

"Indeed, Watson. But let's get to work."

▶ *To investigate the pile of papers, turn to 86.*

▶ *To look in the drinks cabinet, turn to 72.*

▶ *To examine the desk, turn to 39.*

▶ *To sit at the table, turn to 79.*

CAGE

You arrive at the large oblong and find that it is a solid rectangular structure, covered in black fabric. Attached to the fabric is a rope, which ascends into the very top level of the tower. Beyond the oblong is a stage and hundreds of chairs and benches, all set up for the concert in three or four hours' time.

Watson is walking around the structure, examining the fabric. After a few moments he calls to you.

"Here Holmes, there is a slit in the fabric just here. I do believe this is our way in."

You hurry over to join him. Together you move through the fabric's slit and emerge into a corridor of the heavy material. Watson strikes a match to guide you. You stumble your way through the darkness for a couple of moments, and then find yourself at the end of the corridor.

You're at a doorway, and a small silver lock protrudes through a gap in the fabric. You think you can hear a muffled voice or voices just beyond. Odon? You wonder.

Watson hands you the key and you put it into the lock and turn. The door opens. Success! But suddenly there is an almighty clang. A metal gate has fallen behind you. You are now within a cage of criss-crossing metal bars. Seemingly trapped, you try the gate behind you. It is locked, but with an intriguing ancient lock. Curious. You push on through the fabric towards the muffled voice and after a few moments you emerge into an opening. Odon standing in front of you.

▶ *Turn to 95.*

⑨ ON THE WAY TO WATERLOO BARRACKS

from 68

You head quickly across the enclosure towards Waterloo Barracks, just as the late afternoon light catches the side of the vast White Tower. One, two, three ravens flap heavily over, disturbing the air all around you, cawing loudly. The silence after their passage is soothing. You stop for a moment.

In the stillness there seems to be a sweet tinkling music, to the tune of 'London Bridge Is Falling Down, Falling Down, Falling Down' . . . Did you perhaps have one drink too many just now? You catch Watson's eyes.

He moves on. "Come along . . . We have our next destination."

But you pause, as the tune begins again.

▶ *To investigate the music, turn to 73.*

⑩ THIRD PIECE

from 50

"Now this one," you say. "This looks more likely. Then the sequence must be . . ."

Your voice dies to nothing.

Watson moves away, up a step or two. "So many have passed through the Tower, Holmes. Perhaps walked these very stairs . . . Look how they are worn away in the centre by the passage of so many feet. Queen Elizabeth, Gloriana herself, was cooped up in the Tower, as a princess you know. In 1554."

Is he trying to change the subject? Let you down easily?

You can see that you are leading him down a blind alley with this answer. "We must try again," he says.

▶ *Return to 50.*

from 24

You both make your way back across the wide spaces of the Tower enclosure to the Lanthorn Tower, finding your way into an upper room.

"Rather beautifully restored, wouldn't you say?' Watson continues relentlessly: "Fine windows . . ."

You raise your eyebrows questioningly and he continues. "It was restored by Antony Salvin forty-odd years ago after a terrible fire last century."

You hold up a hand to halt the river of historical information and wave forward towards the number design drawn very neatly in chalk on the floor.

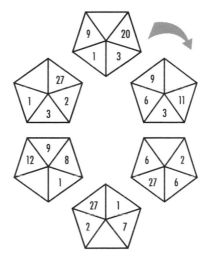

Written on the floor beneath the numbers, you see that opposite faces meet in similar ways and there is something they all share.

Watson begins: "There are six missing numbers, and the arrow at the top indicates moving clockwise around the design, I'd say."

"Bravo," you give a thin smile. "The puzzle should give us a sequence of six numbers and then we need to work out how to convert that into an indication of where to go next."

▶ *Use the code wheel to convert the six numbers into a six-letter word, then turn to the paragraph matching the second number in the sequence.*

FLAGSTONE 1

"I think it's flagstone 1," Watson says. "Which indicates . . ." He looks at the map. ". . . Hmm, slim pickings. I think we need to think again."

▶ *Return to 43.*

IN THE SHRUBBERY

You move towards the shrubbery and, after just a few moments searching, you find another note bearing a short musical phrase. This one has the title 'Sweet'. There is no sign of the flick of hair, or the person the hair belongs to. You stand up with a sigh and start making your way towards the Martin Tower.

"These musical phrases, Holmes," Watson asks, running slightly in an attempt to keep up. "What are they? What do they mean?"

You don't respond. You're not quite sure what to say.

▶ *Turn to 38.*

A MUSICAL NOTE

from 37

Watson is still harrumphing about the need to hurry on to the chapel, but you are focused on the slip of paper. The eerie musical note lingers in your ears. You find a small boulder on the ground, pull it over, and balance on it as you reach up into the branches.

Watson hurries over, agitated. "What are you doing Holmes? There's no time to climb trees, we really do need to get on!"

You ignore Watson's chastising tone and hand him the small, folded piece of paper you retrieved from the branches. Watson looks at you blankly.

"Did you hear a single note held on the violin just a few moments ago, just after your short historical lesson on the history of Tower Green? And your display of devotion to the royal family?"

Not a movement on his face, but he takes the folded paper, opens it and shows it to you.

"Aha," you say, "A musical moment . . ." There is a stave, a sequence of notes and a single word "My".

Watson studies the paper, "No doubt it is a clue, an important message of some sort."

"Exactly, dear Watson."

Contemplating the notes, you find yourself thinking of Odon and his music being played tomorrow. How is he involved in this plot, you wonder? You refold the paper and put it into your pocket.

▶ *Turn to 89.*

TO THE COLDHARBOUR TOWER

"Fifteen," Watson says triumphantly as he completes the magic square.

"That is correct. I have been waiting for you to finish and then inform me what structure is numbered 15 on our map."

"It is the Coldharbour Tower."

This proves to be a long haul, from the Bowyer Tower in the northern wall all the way round the barracks to the centre of the Tower enclosure. You easily outpace Watson, but even you are beginning to feel weary by the time you arrive. And when you get there, the Coldharbour Tower is no more than a ruin.

"Remarkable tale here, Holmes, of the only woman ever to escape from the Tower – a certain Alice Tankerville, reputedly a witch and pirate, no less, imprisoned for the theft of 366 golden crowns. She was kept in strictest confinement in the Coldharbour Tower, but befriended one of her guards and was moments away from leaving London on horseback when the guard was recognized. She didn't last long after that." In the fading light, Watson's eyes are shining with the excitement of the tale.

It is a beautiful evening and undoubtedly atmospheric. You scan the ruins of the tower and the green before it. A spot of white tucked into some crumbling masonry turns out to be paper inscribed with a riddle.

> Ponder your imprisoned state
> Where a fearless pirate maid broke free
> Your next move ever I dictate
> To bring you to disgrace all three
> . . . But you are dawdling . . .
> To move and make the most of time
> Find a body that can hold wine
> And that sunlight might make to shine.

"Cheap rhymes and boasting," you mutter.

"Dreadful man," Watson says. "But what do you think, Holmes? Must be a wine glass – and we know where they are, in plenty? Let's return to the Yeoman Warders' Club."

It could be, but you are not sure.

► *To follow Watson to the Yeoman Warders' Club, turn to 28.*

► *To inspect the other side of the Coldharbour Tower ruins, turn to 77.*

THE CELL

In the Beauchamp Tower Watson leads you into a small room. You cast your eyes around it. The walls are red brick and there are large flagstones beneath your feet. It's surprisingly cold. The heavy wooden door behind you has a small hole in the front, covered with a metal grate. You are under no illusion that this is a cell. Or was a cell. You're not sure what it is to you yet. Your eyes are caught by something scratched in the wall. It's a tally of sorts, a countdown maybe? There is something protruding from between the bricks. You peer closer and see that it's a small, grubby scroll of paper.

Gingerly you extract the scroll from the wall. It's not so dirty as you first thought. In fact, you'd estimate that it has only been there a couple of days, perhaps even just a few hours. You smooth the sheet out and read:

> Holmes, my old foe,
> I've waited a long time for this moment, as you can see – counting down the hours . . . You've walked straight into a prison, in an ancient fortress. You couldn't make it up. It'll all be over in the morning, so while we wait, let's have some fun, eh? Now consider your position. As you know, in a situation like this, sometimes all you can do is . . . pray.
> Yours, M

"Moriarty?" Watson asks.

"Moriarty," you nod.

"He must have survived at the Reichenbach Falls, just as you did, Holmes."

"Of course," you retort, perhaps a little too sharply. "He hinted at it in the previous note: 'Trapped once more and teetering on the brink between life and endless oblivion'."

"As you were at the Falls. Of course. And he's trapped us here." Watson is struggling to keep the fear out of his voice.

"Indeed, he has."

"But why now, Holmes? Why come out of hiding now? And lay a trap for us here?"

"All will become clear, I am sure, Watson. And knowing Moriarty as I do, he'll have left a way through. He'll want to prove only he is up to the challenge."

"Where next, then?" Watson asks. You look at the wall, once again, and an idea begins to formulate.

► *Work out which destination is encoded in the wall tally and head there.*

TO THE CRYPT – "HOLD A MOMENT, HOLMES"

"I have it, of course." You snap your fingers. "We are headed below. Where would you go below from a church? Why, to the crypt of course. And the letter and number clues confirm it. Three shields gives you C for the first letter and 25 tails give you . . ."

"Hold a moment, Holmes," Watson interrupts your crystal-clear reasoning. He is holding up the note again, showing you a second challenge on the reverse:

Royals resting as you were.
Find a guide at thrice three o'clock.

Be sure to flip. Of course. You had to check the back of the note before you could proceed.

"I do believe . . ." Watson says excitedly, ". . . this is a puzzle based on the clock face. Royals resting as you were suggests to me the same coats of arms we were looking at before, so . . . We look in the position of three o'clock . . .?"

"Very good, Watson." You can be magnanimous.

"But there is nothing?"

As usual he needs your help. "What does thrice three o'clock suggest?"

"The same position but the third shield. . . Ah, here we have it!"

The tile in that position is loose, and Watson is able to lift it with his forefinger and thumb. Beneath the tile a circular device has been concealed. He holds it up triumphantly before you.

"A wheel!"

You both examine it carefully. [See the device on the cover.]

"It looks like some kind of translation device? Symbols, letters, colours . . . A code wheel?"

"Very good, Watson. Now let's proceed to the crypt . . ."

▶ *Turn to 22.*

(18) # GBDA

from 46

You play the notes GBDA.

There is a terrible silence in the cage. Your ears strain for the sound of the lock opening – but nothing.

You look around. Odon does not look enthused at your efforts, or comforted by the presence of the Crown Jewels.

You hang your head.

▶ *Turn to 57.*

"E," Watson says.

"Quite right," you answer. "Fascinating thing the SATOR square, not unlike those magical number squares the ancient Chinese went in for so much . . ." It's a kind of verbal lock, you think to yourself. "Yes, locking up or tying down language. Or hiding meaning."

Once again, Watson seems to be attuned to your thoughts in the most curious fashion. "Talking of locks, I heard the most fascinating claim last week about the court musician Mark Smeaton, the fellow who was gaoled and executed as the alleged lover of Anne Boleyn." He stops, chewing his moustache.

"Yes?" you enquire.

"Ah! You do take an interest in my historical knowledge!"

You roll your eyes.

"Well, there is a Tudor-era lock you may have heard of, supposedly one of the most secure ever made. Only one key to it exists. I was told that Smeaton was its inventor, but that it can also be opened by playing a sequence of musical notes." Watson continues: "It was designed, the story goes, so that when King Henry was at his most suspicious Anne could retire for the night under lock and key, with this lock I should say, but Smeaton alone could gain access to her for dalliance!"

Genuinely fascinating, you think. Watson is still talking. "Smeaton famously said it was 'For My Sweet Love'."

"What was?"

Watson is surprised you are maintaining interest. "Eh?" he snorts. "The motets he wrote for her, I think. Or perhaps the lock itself?"

You refocus on the puzzle. What do we do with the answer 19? you think. "We could try taking 19 steps across the floor." You look down. "And look here is an arrow pointing the way." After 19 steps there is a message on the floor and beyond it on the floor a number square. "Ha! Very clever palindromic phrase, but I don't think it applies, Watson. We're being asked to fill in the missing numbers. It looks like a magic square. One space is circled, so it must be our intended destination."

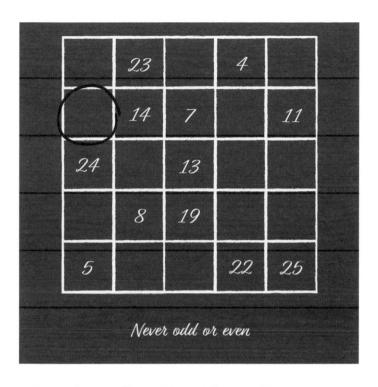

Never odd or even

▶ In a magic square, the sum of the numbers in each row, column and main diagonal must come to the same amount. In this example, each of the 25 squares holds one of the numbers from 1 to 25. Identify the number missing from the circled space, find the numbered location on the map and turn to that number.

TRAITORS' GATE

from 70

"Traitor," you announce. "That must mean Traitors' Gate."

Watson leads the way to the wharf called Traitors' Gate. "Edward I built this tower, St Thomas's Tower, and it originally gave onto the Thames, with a water gate so he could arrive by boat. It became known as Traitors' Gate when Tudor prisoners were delivered by barge . . ."

"Where are you getting all this not-unfamiliar information, Watson?"

He pats what appears to be a book in his pocket. "I've been reading up . . ."

His eyes glaze over. You can tell he is thinking about the tea you were expecting to have at 221B. But your day appears to be heading in a different direction. You look up at the Tower and the famous squatting ravens.

"I say!" he says.

You follow his eyes to see a bottle floating in the Thames with paper extruding from it. You manage to hook it and pull out two pieces of paper.

"It looks as if someone is expecting us to spend a little more time here," you say. "Here is a map of the Tower complex. And a note."

You read aloud:

> Traitors' Gate will prove to have been the right way in for you. I know what you are planning, and the traitors you will be before the night is out. Did your fingers always gravitate towards the shiny? And beware the Bridge by morning. Now look for ammunition. Follow the letter you find at the bottom right when all move, when T is touching only P and A and the leftmost two are not capital. You will i Am sure come out on top. Remember: keep the structure steady.

"Traitor! What on earth?" Watson puzzles. "Something shiny?"

Your attention is focused most on the threat. You look up at Tower Bridge. *Beware the Bridge by morning* . . . that is when the concert is scheduled, is it not?

"Follow the letter . . . " you mutter. "I say, do you think he could be referring to these cannonballs?"

"We need to rearrange them," Watson grunts as he tries to lift one.

"In our mind's eye, surely, old man . . ." You look closer. "I think we pick one letter as our next destination. And looking at the map I would say we have a choice of "T" - St Thomas's Tower, right here. I'd also say the Postern Gate. Queen's Stairs could be 'q', which is also on the wharf."

"What about 'A' and 'i'?"

"We discount them. Do you not see the tiny crosses beneath them in the note?"

▶ *You will find the map at the back of this book.*
To go to the Postern Gate, turn to 65.

▶ *To go to St Thomas's Tower, turn to 80.*

▶ *To go to the Queen's Stairs, turn to 33.*

THE ADVENTURE OF THE TOWER OF LONDON

(21) TO THE WINDOW (LANTHORN TOWER)

from 11

"It spells W-I-N-D-O-W." You lead the way across and inspect the frames carefully. They are metal with a lattice design and small curved handles for opening. Written in chalk on the stone beneath them, you read: 'F > o > r > w > a > r > d'.

What can that mean? How can you go forward when facing a window? Clamber through? Forward on the map, perhaps?

"We could try opening the window," Watson suggests. "That could be said to be going forward."

"Locked," you say.

"Look again," he replies, "Are you sure?"

You manage to open the window and find hanging from the outside of the handle a long thread on which is suspended a cotton bag containing a note.

"It reads JHW, SH," you say. Your initials – and Watson's. You hand Watson the paper.

"Look, Holmes," he says. "There is an addition below: Sherlock Always Look Twice."

"I think I see where this is going," you say, "and where we should be going next."

▶ *Decode the message to find your next destination on the map. Turn to the number that matches it there.*

JHW, SH

Sherlock Always Look Twice

IN THE CRYPT

Down into the crypt you go, slipping the code wheel into your pocket.

"I happen to know, Holmes, that this crypt contains the remains of Lt-Col John Gurwood, the fellow who edited the *Dispatches of the Duke of Wellington*. I would have liked to pick his brains . . ."

"Stop, Watson," you breathe, just inside the doorway. There is a haunting chill in the crypt. Perhaps natural in a place of burial.

But he carries on, almost as if he was attuned to your thoughts: "After her beheading, Anne Boleyn was buried in the chapel upstairs. Her remains were discovered in the chapel when it was being renovated and brought to the crypt. And do you know her headless ghost has been seen . . ."

"Hush," you whisper. "Look."

Footsteps chalked on the floor lead to a marked spot. You follow them and survey the scene. "I think," you say, "we have found an immediate use for our code wheel." A series of designs are visible in the room. "We are being communicated with."

"To what purpose?"

"It seems the Professor is testing our ability to follow a trail of his devising through the Tower. Doubtless more of his scheme will be revealed. For now let's decode this message and work out our next destination."

▶ *Use the map to go to the location you discover.*

TRAPPED

You reach out towards brick 23 and push it gently. The brick moves with ease, joining the sun, the moon, lightning and flames in their position set back from the wall.

You experience a moment of elation, shattered almost immediately by a deafening clang and clash. Your chosen brick has released the rusty portcullis gate, which has fallen from the sky above. It now stands between you and the outside world. So much for defunct!

Watson looks at you with terror in his eyes. "We're trapped, Holmes!" he exclaims. "How on earth did we get here? Surely this could have been avoided? We have allowed ourselves to walk straight into a cage!"

You nod.

"Mind you," Watson assures himself, "the Tower of London is a busy place with many guards in residence and there should be plenty of people around who can help us . . ."

"Of course I was aware that getting trapped was a possibility, Watson, but someone seems to be set on bringing us inside. Perhaps we should focus more on solving that mystery than on trying to escape," you respond. Watson is silent. He doesn't look entirely convinced.

You survey the scene and spy a small, smudged envelope tied to one of the bars of the portcullis. You go to open it. A note inside reads:

> Well, look where we find
> ourselves . . .
> Trapped once more and teetering
> on the brink between life
> and endless oblivion.
> Welcome to the Bloody Tower.
> Take the stairs, Holmes.
> Drip, drip, drip . . .
> Who knows what blood may be
> spilled before tonight is out.

You sigh. You've already had quite enough of these smug little riddles. You start towards the stairs.

"What do you think he means, Holmes, 'Once again teetering on the brink between life and endless oblivion'?"

You almost correct Watson on his assumption, but then stop yourself. Of course it's a he. It could only ever be one person.

Together you set off towards the stairs.

▶ *Turn to 60.*

FLINT TOWER

You make your way to Flint Tower. At the top of the winding staircase is a substantial room with a large wooden desk beneath a window and three battered wooden chairs. Watson sits in one with a sigh, blowing his breath through his bushy moustache. You wonder again why he insists on such an unnecessary, uncomfortable and frankly unsightly addition to his face.

Meanwhile he is speaking: "What a wonderful old place the Tower is."

You stand looking out the window at the large enclosure and its many buildings. It is a beautiful autumn evening; you listen to the harsh call of the ravens.

"I say! Here's another map," Watson exclaims, looking at the desk.

You stand beside him. "Not exactly," you tell him. "It's more like another challenge." There are no fewer than nine towers on the plan, each with a word beneath it.

"What do you make of this, Holmes?" He reads the names: Bowyer, Brick, Flint, Devereux . . . Names of towers? You wonder.

You compare it to the layout on the main map of the complex and, sure enough, each is the same as one of the towers. One tower is marked END. And the others have directional instructions.

"Well, we have the end marked, Holmes," he points out. "That's our next destination. It's the Flint Tower. Not a puzzle at all, just simple instructions."

"We are in the Flint Tower at this very moment," you say gently.

"Ah, just so," he murmurs rather sheepishly.

"Look here," you say. Written on the plan are the words *Where to? Where from?* You note again the directional instructions within each tower.

You ponder. "Should we be working our way backwards, perhaps, to find out where you start from to get to this 'end'?"

"And that would be our next destination?" he asks, running his finger triumphantly across that monstrous moustache.

Now you have it. Yes. You both set to work.

▶ *Find the correct starting point, look it up upon the map and turn to that paragraph.*

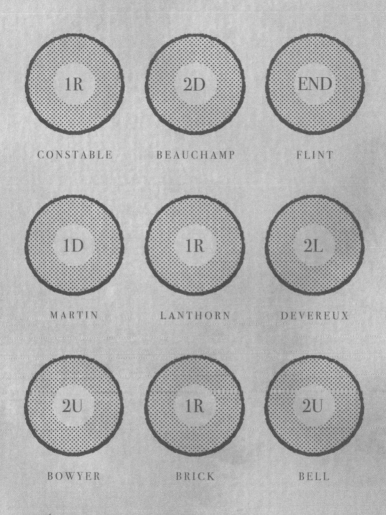

CONSTABLE · 1R

BEAUCHAMP · 2D

FLINT · END

MARTIN · 1D

LANTHORN · 1R

DEVEREUX · 2L

BOWYER · 2U

BRICK · 1R

BELL · 2U

Where to?
Where from?

WELL TOWER

You make your way to the Well Tower.

"So called," burbles Watson, "because it guarded the well."

"You amaze me." You look eagerly around.

"Holmes, we have been to almost every destination at the Tower of London," Watson says, "and we're yet to find Odon or any way to stop this morning's threat. We must try and find a way out to prevent whatever is planned to take place on the Bridge."

You close the door behind you, to find a note pinned to its inner surface.

"There is a final puzzle somewhere in the room, Watson. Let's get to work." You scan the room. It is bare. Not a clue. No hidden messages.

"I'm not so sure, Holmes. Perhaps Moriarty wants us to be stuck here, looking across rather helplessly at the Bridge?"

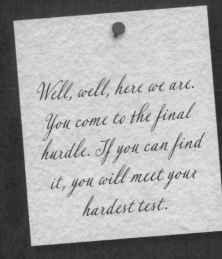

Well, well, here we are. You come to the final hurdle. If you can find it, you will meet your hardest test.

From the window, you see Watson is right: there is a fine but, in the circumstances, rather troubling view of the Bridge. You look down at the wharf, at the river on which so many prisoners were delivered to the Tower . . . to meet their end.

Yet at the back of your mind, something knocks. Is there something you read earlier that can help you now?

"Where is the well, Watson? It's not marked on the map."

He looks at you quizzically.

Is it worth going to investigate the well? Or should you stay in the room to prove you can overcome Moriarty's challenge?

▶ *To stay in the tower and carry on looking, turn to 91.*

▶ *To look for the well, turn to 30.*

㉖ THE ROBES

from 88

Watson consults the map. "I believe we should be heading to the North Bastion," he says.

You don't move.

"Some of these letters in the note are emboldened," he explains, "and I do believe they spell out the word blue; the colour of the angel's robes." Even he doesn't sound particularly convinced.

You remain immobile.

He gives up by himself and sighs.

You don't hear it, however. Watson's ramblings have given you a fresh idea. You return to the painting for another look.

▶ *Return to 88.*

ALL'S WELL THAT ENDS WELL
– AT 221B

"More tea, my dear? Perhaps a scone?" Mrs Hudson is treating Odon like an old friend.

Meanwhile, he is speaking. "After I wrote to you, Sherlock, and received no response, I came up with a rather more intriguing plan, involving taking and returning your Stradivarius – rest assured I treated it most carefully – to attract your attention. I knew if I could engage your attention you would help. But then Moriarty and Andor took matters into their own hands, hoping to disgrace you and me at the same time."

"But the haunting notes we heard at the Tower?" you ask. "You were under lock and key at the time?"

Odon smiles mysteriously. "My accomplice, seeing that I had been taken captive, had to work alone. She found the secret of the lock," he chuckles, "And shared it with you. When you entered the cage I thought we were done for. I had no idea about the lock's musical secret."

"Why didn't your – accomplice – simply pass me the information I needed?" Watson asks Odon.

You reply: "Oh come on, Watson. We never can be sure who is watching from the shadows."

"What a thing of beauty the lock is," Watson says. "I had heard the stories, of course, about Mark Smeaton and Anne Boleyn, but always assumed they were myths."

"We don't know, though," you add, "whether the lock really was made by Smeaton."

"But surely, Holmes, MSAB?" Watson continues to clarify: "Mark Smeaton, Anne Boleyn?"

"Oh, come on," Mrs H says. "Allow a little romance into your life."

You prefer to reserve judgement.

"Well," Odon chuckles, "as the Bard says, 'All's well that ends well'."

"Perhaps a glass of port to toast that all has 'ended well'?" Watson smiles.

You drink to Watson's toast and peruse the reports of your adventure.

THE END

The Evening Gazette

23 September 1896

HOLMES FOILS PLOT ON TOWER BRIDGE, SCHEMING VILLAIN IN CUSTODY

BAKER STREET'S FINEST HALTS DARING ATTEMPT TO STEAL CROWN JEWELS

HER MAJESTY 'DELIGHTED' AS DETECTIVE SAVES CELEBRATION CONCERT AND UNCOVERS ATTEMPT TO FRAME COMPOSER

Our proud country's most brilliant detective, Sherlock Holmes, triumphed once again today, foiling a dastardly plot at London's Tower Bridge involving the attempted theft of the Crown Jewels, and unmasking Brother Andor von Mihalovic of the Pannonhalma Abbey in Hungary as an unscrupulous villain. In doing so, Holmes also stopped Andor's attempt to frame his brother, the composer Odon von Mihalovic, and uncovered a scheme involving notorious criminal mastermind Professor James Moriarty – whom many had assumed to be dead – to sell off many of the historic riches from the Abbey's celebrated library. (Continued on page 3.)

(Continued on page 3.)

SECRET OF 'MUSICAL' TUDOR LOCK DISCOVERED

A unique musical Tudor lock that opens when the correct sequence of notes is played was used by the kidnappers and thieves in this scheme. Previously the lock was thought to be operated by key – and only a single key remained in existence. The lock was said to have been invented by court musician Mark Smeaton, who was the alleged lover of Queen Anne Boleyn and was executed at the Tower on 17 May 1536.

HALLÉ ORCHESTRA SHINES, NORMAN-NERUDA MAGNIFICENT

The foiling of the plot allowed Hungarian composer Odon von Mihalovic's sublime orchestral piece 'Sweet Thames Run Softly' to be performed to a select audience, including Queen Victoria, to celebrate Her Majesty today becoming Britain's longest-ruling monarch. The Hallé Orchestra was simply magnificent, and a solo performed by violinist Wilhelmine Norman-Neruda was exemplary, her haunting notes thrilling in the autumn air. The soloist surprised onlookers by saying, "I am delighted that Mr Holmes was able to be here today."

TALES OF GIANT RAT OF SUMATRA CAUSE PANIC, SHIP LOST

The loss of the *Matilda Briggs* and hair-raising tales of attacks on sailors by the giant rat of Sumatra are circulating at the Port of London. Asked by our reporter about the incident, with which he is known to have become involved, Sherlock Holmes said, "it is a story for which the world is not yet prepared."

BACK TO THE YEOMAN WARDERS' CLUB

Watson leads the way enthusiastically back across the greensward. You wonder if what he is really interested in is further alcoholic refreshment. You arrive to find a glass containing a note in the grass beside the doors.

"Look, Holmes," Watson says, brandishing the paper. "Was this here before?"

He reads it aloud: "Sober up, Dr Watson. Licensing hours are over. Better head back."

► *Return to 15.*

TIED IN KNOTS

"The correct entrance point is 29," you say, gesturing for Watson to hand you the map.

He doesn't move. "I'm not sure Holmes, you know," he says, after a moment. "I believe starting at 29 means you end up stuck."

You follow his finger as he maps out the route and realize Watson is indeed correct. You step away and sigh. You are indeed stuck. How are you here again? Encircled by Moriarty, chasing his cryptic threats. You wander to one of the small window slits and peer out, considering John Arden and John Gerard's rope-based escape. You'd never be able to throw a rope into the tower, you think. The hole is too small, too precise, but perhaps you'd be able to throw one out?

You ponder the thought for a moment and then return to the maze to map your way through once more.

► *Turn to 56.*

WELL TUNNEL

Around the corner from the Well Tower you find the well, boarded up. Watson wrenches off the wooden covering to reveal steps going down.

"Should we?" asks Watson.

You nod and lead the way down.

You reach the bottom of the steps and begin to move quickly. The tunnels are narrow, musty and clearly very old.

"Can you hear that, old chap?" Watson asks, grabbing your arm.

"What?"

You stop for a moment to listen. "It sounds like an animal, coming after us."

Watson begins to run and you follow him. The sounds, whether of a beast or just the croaking old tunnels, get louder and more intense. There are moments where you are sure something is right behind you and then you turn around to find nothing.

After a couple of moments, you arrive, panting, at a fork in your path.

"Let's go right!" Watson shouts and begins to start off down the pathway. You pull him back.

"Look here," you say, pointing at something stamped into the dirt. It's a scrambled message of sorts. The writing is from a hand you don't recognize and just below there are initials, 'M' and an 'S', and a date, 1536. The coded message reads:

YIIK MAX MATFXL, ZII EXYM

Below the 'Y', someone has added an 'F'.

"These tunnels must have been crafted during the Tudor reign," Watson says with awe. "I wonder how many others have escaped down this path."

Another howl from the tunnels returns you to the task at hand, and you set about decoding the message.

▶ *If you think you should turn left, turn to 62.*

▶ *If you think you should turn right, turn to 64.*

TO THE MARTIN TOWER

from 58

Together you rush towards the Martin Tower. With every passing moment the sun gets warmer and time for you to escape gets shorter.

Watson is humming next to you as you walk, or is the humming you? Or is it in the air?

You stop for a moment. Watson is agitated, "Come on, Holmes!" he calls. "We've got no time."

You listen intently. "What is that, Watson?" you ask. "That sequence of notes again and again. Have we heard it? Is it in my mind?" Watson stops and listens, too.

"Where is it coming from, Holmes?" he asks.

You stand still, close your eyes, to tune your ears into its location, then quickly you turn away from the Tower, towards some bushes, and point. "I believe it's over there."

Watson rushes towards the bushes with a little too much enthusiasm. He dives in, surfacing moments later with the fourth Stradivarius string. He holds it aloft, like a trophy, before catching himself and passing it to you.

You are distracted, staring at some shrubs in the middle distance, where you are sure you can see branches moving, and perhaps, even, a flick of human hair?

"What on earth?" you exclaim, moving towards the shrubbery. Watson almost grabs you.

"We've no time!" he says, gesturing to the sun in the absence of a timepiece. "We have the final string. Come on, Holmes!" He is correct. Although . . .

▶ *To walk towards the shrubs, turn to 13.*

▶ *To continue to the Martin Tower, turn to 38.*

ATTIC STORES

Watson follows you up three flights of stairs and, eventually, you climb into the attic. Here, you find a lit gas lamp awaiting you. It's odd, all these indications that someone is here, guiding you, but you're yet to see a soul, except those glimpses of red-gold hair.

You glance around the room, which holds an indiscriminate collection of objects from around the site, and from throughout the Tower's history. Books, china and glassware, some rusty armour. In the corner you can see a full set of theatre costumes and at your feet are a number of cheap glass gems, coloured to look like emeralds and rubies. Stuck in the gems is an envelope. 'My worthy adversary' is written on the front, the word 'worthy' crossed out. Cheap, even by Moriarty's standards.

Watson is standing at the other end of the room, looking out at Tower Bridge, looming over the river in the reddening sunset. You open the letter and read out loud:

"So you pick me up from amongst the gems . . . Let's hope none of them make their way into your pockets, Mr Holmes . . . Who knows what you'll be found with before the night is out, or when the morning comes."

You look up at Watson but he is still staring out across the water. You return to the letter: "I'll catch you, Holmes. You'll be listening to Odon's music from behind the bars. There's nothing you can do about it. As the Thames runs softly . . . and you're caught red-handed . . . and I'll have it all."

You sigh. These letters are so self-regarding. It's clear something terrible is meant to happen tomorrow, and Moriarty feels he has the upper hand, but how does it relate to the concert; what does he expect to catch you doing?

▶ *Turn to 75.*

(33) QUEEN'S STAIRS

You lead the way along the quayside, away from Tower Bridge, to the Queen's Stairs. Steep steps run down into the river. It was clearly a historic entrance to the Tower complex when most important visitors arrived by barge or boat.

"I believe Anne Boleyn disembarked here, when she was crowned . . ." Watson breathes heavily behind you, having been hurrying to keep up, yet continues to speak. ". . . And when she was to be executed."

Your eyes flick across his perspiring face and scan the area. There is no evidence of a message or visual alert from whoever is communicating with you. You must have been mistaken. You turn away and set off.

"Holmes?"

"Back to the Traitors' Gate, Watson."

▶ *Return to 20.*

(34) FOURTH PIECE

"Of the four, I would plump for this one," Watson says.

"But why?" you say sharply. "What would the reasoning be behind that?"

"Well," he pauses, "perhaps . . ."

"Perhaps, nothing," you snap. "Come on, buck up, Watson."

He shuffles uncomfortably. You note how the steps of the ancient staircase are worn away in the centre, making them a good deal more dangerous to use.

▶ *Return to 50.*

STORES

Watson leads the way eastwards, to the Stores. He pushes open the door and you walk in together. The large building is cavernous and appears to be deserted.

Your destination within the building and your intended task are not immediately clear, so you begin to explore the ground floor. Outside, the sun is setting and the last light is beautiful, but in this shadowy interior it is gloomy and you light the gas lamps as you go, illuminating one room after another.

Watson is surprisingly silent. The Stores are history-free, and human-free and everything-else free, apparently. You are growing exasperated and are about to turn to Watson and ask if there is any way you could have made a mistake, when something catches your eye – a large sack of grain leaning against a wall. The grain itself isn't confusing, but the weight listed on the label reads a measly 26oz.

You gesture for Watson to come and join you.

"Look here, 26oz for this great sack. That can't be correct, can it?" you ask, turning towards him. "What on earth would lead somebody to mislabel their grain quite so incorrectly?"

"And these, Holmes," Watson says, indicating a number of smaller bags piled up against another wall. "20oz, 7oz, 19oz . . . absolutely none of these are correct!"

"Perhaps they are trying to lead us somewhere? Show us something?" Watson asks.

"1, 7, 19, 20, 20, 26, 26, 26," you read aloud. "What can that mean?"

▶ *Use the map to find your next location.*

HEADING TO WAKEFIELD TOWER

from 41

You make your way out of the Constable Tower and begin to cross the courtyard outside. The dawn breeze is strong and quick and whistles past your ears. It is still three-quarters dark.

Then, for just a moment it sounds like more than the breeze. For an instant you are certain you can hear a single haunting note being played on the violin.

Watson grabs your arm. So he can hear it, too?

The note dies away but the sound of it echoes in your memory. The playing, the ghostly, haunting tone almost reminds you of something, of someone you've heard play before. You can't place who.

"Shall we go to investigate?" you ask, moving towards the music. Something cold and hard reaches out of the darkness and traces its way down your face. You jump backwards.

"What's up old chap?" Watson turns, concerned.

You look up and breathe a sigh of relief. You had walked straight into another Stradivarius string. You detach it from the tree branch above and pocket it quickly. The memory of the note echoes in your ears. Or? Perhaps? Is it being played once more? You take a few tentative steps into the darkness.

Watson falters, unsure. "We have no sense of the time, Holmes. We've been asleep for hours. Don't you think we should get on?"

You pause and consider his words.

▶ *To heed Watson's warning and make your way to the Wakefield Tower, turn to 49.*

▶ *To follow the music, turn to 74.*

HEADING TO ST PETER'S

from 16

From the tally code, you worked out easily enough that your next destination is the Chapel of St Peter ad Vincula. As you lead the way there, using the map, Watson calls to you to pause.

"Where is everyone, Holmes? Why have we seen no one in the Tower?"

You look around, wondering.

He is speaking again: "Here on what they call Tower Green was a place of execution – no lesser name than Anne Boleyn and also Catherine Howard, two queens of England, were beheaded here . . . this area of granite paving was laid by our own dear queen, Victoria, to mark the spot." He shivers, mumbling: "For dust thou art and unto dust thou shalt return."

There is a surprising mildness in the autumn air and you feel the sun come from behind a cloud, warm on your face. In this moment of stillness you hear what sounds like a single note played on a violin. Haunting.

Your eyes follow the note and land on a thin cord catching the light beneath a tree at the side of the green. "Look at this," you call to Watson, "is there a wire or a cord moving there in the breeze?"

You cover the ground swiftly with your long stride. When you get a little closer, your keen eyes see something all too familiar.

"Quite remarkable Watson, it's a violin string." It puts you in mind, as perhaps it's supposed to, of your missing Stradivarius, which disappeared last week. You detach the string from the tree and pocket it. Turning back to Watson, your eye is caught by something white, a scroll of paper perhaps? It's a little higher up in the tree, just out of reach.

Watson is in a hurry. "Come now, old man," he says, "let's get on to the next challenge. We're stuck here in this place, with so many reminders of death and the passing of time. And your greatest foe laying traps for us . . ."

He is hurrying away.

▶ *To ignore Watson and move back to the tree, turn to 14.*

▶ *To agree with Watson and move on to the Chapel of St Peter ad Vincula, turn to 55.*

MARTIN TOWER

You rush towards the Martin Tower. The light illuminating your path no longer has the fuzzy glow of dawn. It is morning and you are still stuck in the Tower. In the full light of day the reality of your situation hits you.

As you approach the door, a single cloud passes over the sun, casting a shadow on your path. You shiver and flinch. Watson chuckles.

"This Tower is rumoured to be haunted by the ghost of a black bear," he explains. "I didn't put you down as the type to believe in ghosts, Holmes." He continues. "In fact they had a whole menagerie here at one time: elephants, leopards and even a polar bear."

You keep moving. There's no time for this. You push open the door. In the centre of the floor is a small envelope. You open it and read:

> *Here we are, Holmes. We have met our denouement.*
> *Everyone is trapped.*
> *Your dear Odon is trapped. He'll be revealed as a traitor to the Crown and disgraced.*
> *You are trapped here, powerless to do anything to stop it, beaten by my intellect.*
> *And I'll be trapped with a lifetime of riches and the knowledge that I have beaten you. Tally ho, old chap,*
> *M*

You sigh. None of this is quite new information, but to see it all written down, and realize quite how far you are from your target, winds you slightly.

"Come on Holmes, there is something you should see here," Watson calls over to you, bringing you back to the room. "We haven't time."

Watson is right, you haven't. You walk over to join him.

▶ *Turn to 63.*

THE DESK

"I imagine the Constable's desk could be a mine of useful information," Watson says, leading the way across the room.

But when you get there, the top is quite clear. The drawers down the sides are all locked, and the central drawer contains only one document – a newspaper clipping.

LEADING MUSICIANS SERENADE HER MAJESTY

Wednesday's much-anticipated concert on Tower Bridge will feature an orchestra of some of Europe's finest instrumentalists personally invited to perform the world première of Odon von Mihalovic's piece 'Sweet Thames Run Softly' with the Hallé Orchestra in front of Queen Victoria. Among those playing will be the celebrated violinist Wilhelmine Norman-Neruda. Mihalovic will be in the audience and the conductor will be no less a figure than Edward Elgar.

"Neruda!" you shout. "I know her playing. Her attack and bowing are splendid. Her tone is haunting. How satisfactory. We must make sure we unpick whatever scheme Moriarty has laid in our way so we can congratulate Odon and enjoy the concert . . ."

"Ah, Holmes. I wonder how Odon is embroiled in this plot. You don't suppose he is locked up somewhere in the Tower?"

You are not able to find any further information on the desk.

► *To investigate the pile of papers, turn to 86.*

► *To look in the drinks cabinet, turn to 72.*

► *To sit at the table, turn to 79.*

Watson has returned to the curious old lock in the metal gate and is considering it with an intense gaze. You go over to join him. "See here, Holmes, it's these letters again: MSAB."

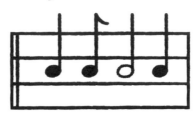

Above the letters there is a short sequence of notes.

"I do wonder, Holmes, whether perhaps our musical friend has in fact been helping us after all . . ."

He continues, "Goodness Holmes, you don't think this can be the lock?"

You are already adding strings to your Stradivarius. Odon joins you and inspects the lock, too.

"MSAB," he reads aloud. "Perhaps Mark Smeaton, Anne Boleyn?" He sighs. "As he locked me in, Moriarty told me you'd join me here and that this lock would be triggered. It is thought to be the most complex and secure lock ever to have been invented, and there is only one key. We are well and truly stuck!"

You begin to tune the strings. Your mind is slipping back through the night, gathering notes on paper, and encoded letters. You are finding your tune.

You turn to Odon: "There might only be one key, but there is more than one way out." You begin to play.

▶ *To play the notes EFGB, turn to 4.*

▶ *To play the notes FDGB, turn to 92.*

▶ *To play the notes GBDA, turn to 18.*

FIRST LIGHT

from 79

You wake with a start. You had a dream that there was someone in the room with you and Watson, talking to you in a rather superior way. Watson is already stirring.

"Just had a moment's shut-eye, Holmes."

"More than a moment, Watson," you say, indicating first light of dawn just visible in the sky outside through the windows.

"What? Look! It's the beginnings of dawn! How long did we sleep?! Time is against us, Holmes. Why didn't you wake me?"

You clear your throat and look down.

What's this? You are both covered with sheets of newspaper as if someone had laid paper blankets over your sleeping bodies. The same on Watson. "Did you do this, Watson?" You ask. He shakes his head morosely. Could someone have been in the room with you? There is a crossword here that has been drawn on the newspaper. And four letters of the answers are ringed.

▶ *Complete the crossword. The four ringed letters form a word well-suited to your current condition and is also the first part of the name of your destination.*

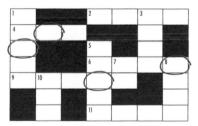

Down
1 There are many on this site
3 Silvery-grey metal
5 Creeps up on you when you're tired
7 Will you be ___ time tomorrow?
8 Fortress
10 You only have to do this to receive help

Across
2 Sleepy
4 Fool; person who rests when they should be looking for clues
6 Adds security
9 Guardian of the Tower
11 For when the Queen arrives

(42) JUST A DROP

from 68

Watson lunges for the first glass, but you pull him back. His pint splashes onto the table and a few drops land inside one of the empty wine glasses.

"I don't think that can be correct," you say. You help him back into an upright position.

You consider the pub. It doesn't look as though anyone has been rushed out of here, shocked or ambushed. All is as expected. What can Moriarty have said? What strings has he pulled? Where has everyone gone? You cast your mind to tomorrow morning. Moriarty's threats land in a different way with the knowledge that the support of the Tower guards has all but disappeared.

You glance at Watson, who has a reddish tinge growing on the sliver of flesh visible above his moustache. It will have to be up to you, you think, nonplussed. You return to the task at hand.

► *Return to 68.*

(43) OUTSIDE THE WATERLOO BARRACKS

from 52

"Step lively, man!" you urge. Is Watson dragging along behind because you've thrust the Strad case into his arms?

But he's stopped altogether. "Hold on, Holmes. Look at this."

On the flagstones outside the Barracks a puzzle has been drawn.

"I say, these are the symbols from the wheel, are they not?" he queries.

One flagstone has been lifted out of position and there are three choices for a replacement, leant against the wall. And there is a note.

Remarkable the trouble Moriarty has gone to with these challenges. He's evidently been looking forward to locking horns again . . . Or is there another reason . . . Is the aim to slow you both up?

"Clearly we are supposed to work out which of the three stones completes the sequence," you note. "But what does the note say?"

Top-down right pair indicate future path.

"The two symbols in the right-hand squares indicate our next destination?" asks Watson.

"With the upper symbol first. You're catching up, Watson."

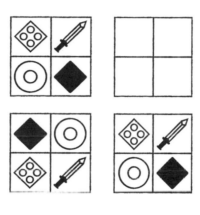

► *If you think the right choice is flagstone 1, turn to 12.*

► *If you think the right choice is flagstone 2, turn to 47.*

► *If you think the right choice is flagstone 3, turn to 67.*

WHITE TOWER

You cast your eyes around at the scene in front of you. Watson is still kindly carrying the stringless Stradivarius in its case.

What's this? A few last rays of early evening sunshine catch on something in the foliage. You see a glint. There's the bottle, hidden in the bushes. You tell Watson. Picking it up he finds a piece of paper stuffed inside.

The paper states: '14 SE William's Tower'.

"William's Tower? Well –" he begins. You are a couple of steps ahead of him. Elementary, you think. He continues: "The White Tower was begun by William the Conqueror in about 1078, as we all know, and SE could be southeast. But how would we know precisely the directions?"

You have the map in your hand. "Really, Watson. Did you not take note of the small compass drawn on the map?"

"Well, I did not. But I see it now," he grumbles.

You both make your way over to the White Tower and carefully pace out 14 steps to the southeast of the great Norman keep.

You show him the map. "We are standing here," you say, "with the Stores to the East, the Main Guard to the West. South is the Lanthorn Tower."

You look up. What now? There is a message spelled out here somehow. You were led here by the one in the bottle, now there is one on the building to direct your next move.

"Pleasant breeze, Holmes," Watson murmurs, "coming straight towards us. And rather helpful."

You scratch your head. What does Watson mean? Is he a step ahead of you for once?

▶ *Work out where to go next.*

DEVEREUX TOWER STOREY 1

from 88

Following the map, you find your way to the Devereux Tower.

You enter a large chamber, sparsely furnished. There is a hard wooden bed, a chair and a badly worn rug.

Your sharp eyes spot a tiny corner of paper tucked beneath the rug and you pull out a note.

> I leave this note in desperation and hope to find a friendly reader. I write with a broken heart – and a blunt pencil on a scrap of paper in captivity. My brother Andor, in alliance with a notorious international criminal, is poised to defraud the great Pannonhalma Abbey, where he resides as a Benedictine, of the immense riches in its library. He tried to involve me in the plot but I secretly determined to use the opportunity given me by having my music performed at Tower Bridge before England's Queen to expose him and his partner in crime – Moriarty. But they found out my plan and I have been swept off the streets in London and kept under lock and key in this tower by a brawny man they call Moran.
>
> Help me!
> Odon von Mihalovic

Watson's gaze is appalled. You nod. "We could have acted sooner. But all we can do now is solve this problem and help Odon out of his crisis. Odon must be somewhere else in the compound. We must find him and prevent whatever Moriarty has planned for Tower Bridge this morning."

After a careful search you find no further clues or hidden documents in the room. You look for a way out – and take a spiral stone staircase that leads to the storey above. As you are climbing, your foot catches on a loose flagstone.

► *To continue up the staircase, turn to 76.*

► *To investigate the flagstone, turn to 81.*

⒋₆ BRICK 46

from 80

You reach out to push brick 46. Watson grabs your hand.

"Are you sure, Holmes?" he asks.

You falter, and let your hand fall to your side. You explain aloud: "I had thought I was being led to the beasts below, somewhere here in the flames," you say, gesturing to the lowest line of bricks.

Watson nods. He lets you continue speaking, "But it doesn't quite bring everything together, does it?"

Watson shakes his head. His manner is nothing short of infuriating.

You consider the message once more, gods above, beasts below, moon, sun, flames, lightning. What direction is this puzzle leading you in?

► *Return to 80.*

FLAGSTONE 2

from 43

"I plump for flagstone 2," you say confidently, although you're actually feeling rather confused. You did both swallow quite a few drinks in the Yeoman Warders' Club.

Watson's now mumbling: "In which case the letters are G, E. Jolly good," he says, "G, E . . . well there is the Gentleman Gaoler's House . . ."

He sets off, a little unsteadily.

But you are having second thoughts. Your head is clearing. "Hold fast, Watson, let's reconsider."

▶ *Return to 43.*

BOWYER TOWER

from 67

Following red you find your way to the Bowyer Tower.

"I'm still not sure I quite understand?" Watson looks at you quizzically, again.

"Well," you explain. "The highest

```
R O T A S
O P X R A
T X N E T
A R X P O
S A T O R
```

number red might reveal is 22. This would combine with the other letters and numbers to give you a maximum of 98. If you'd chosen green or blue, you could have got 25 or 26, which would have given you a total over 100."

Watson nods, seeming satisfied.

You look around and spot curious graffiti on a fragment of the original wall.

"Maybe written by a prisoner . . ." muses Watson.

"It looks like the SATOR palindromic square," you say. "You know that, Watson? But a slightly different form . . . I don't think it was written by a prisoner because one letter is missing in three places, marked with an 'X'."

Obviously, we're still being toyed with by our host.

▶ *Work out which letter is missing, convert it to a number using the code wheel and turn to that number.*

THE LOST LETTER

from 36, 74

You start again for the Wakefield Tower. Heading back past the Constable Tower, your eye is caught. There is something on the wall you didn't notice before. You find a wire letterbox, holding a single unopened letter.

You call Watson over. "This letter is from Odon, addressed to the Constable, postmarked about a month ago. It must have sat here unopened."

Watson nods. You slide the letter out of the envelope and read aloud:

> *Constable,*
>
> *I write to you with a sincere request. I am in dire need of protection.*
>
> *In one month's time I will attend a concert on London's Tower Bridge. I plan to use this concert as a platform.*
>
> *My brother, known as Brother Andor, will soon gain control of Hungary's Pannonhalma Abbey. He plans to profit from the Abbey's riches, to sell off the priceless art and artefacts the Abbey holds for his own personal gain. I will use the concert to let the world know of his plan. However, I cannot do this without support. Andor will try to stop me, I need your help to stop him.*

You sigh. Watson looks at you and turns over the envelope.

"This date," he says, "is about when Odon asked for your help." You nod.

"Despite this letter being unopened," you say, "I am convinced Andor indeed found out. I believe he has trapped Odon. We must save him."

▶ *Turn to 96.*

AT THE BELL TOWER WINDOW

from 5

"B-E-L-L," you call out.

Watson leads the way along the inner wall from the Wakefield Tower. The heavy door at the bottom of the Bell Tower creaks as he hauls it open. He climbs up the steep, narrow stairway, then halts on a small landing.

"Hold a minute, Holmes. Rather beautiful handiwork." He indicates a small stained-glass window set in the tower wall. You examine it. One piece is missing from the design and four pieces are laid on the sill below.

You see quickly that it is not actually a window but a metal grid into which sixteen glass pieces have been fitted. You point this out to him.

"Four by four makes sixteen, with one missing makes fifteen," he muses. "And perhaps take away four on the windowsill from that total? Eleven. Any significance in that?"

Your mind is at work. The designs in the makeshift window are familiar from the code wheel. And on the sill you find 'Spin the wheel' written very neatly in chalk.

You explain the task at hand: work out which of the designs on the sill would logically fit in the design as the missing piece. Then use the wheel to find the next destination.

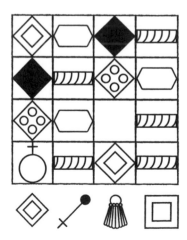

▶ *If you think it is the first piece, turn to 88.*

▶ *If you think it is the second piece, turn to 78.*

▶ *If you think it is the third piece, turn to 10.*

▶ *If you think it is the fourth piece, turn to 34.*

(51) SALT TOWER CHIMNEY – A NOTE

"Aha! Another note!" exclaims Watson. "I must have been right. . ." But his words fade away to silence.

He screws up the paper and throws it to the floor.

It states:

> Woeful, Watson. Hopeless, Holmes. I am happy for you to be cooped up here. You have many worthy forerunners . . . But don't you want to at least try to use your intelligence? I know you are not fathers but if you were where would you look for your baby?

Watson looks really dispirited.

"Come along," you say, "let's give it a second go. We can manage it. In any case this clue gives us a strong indication."

▶ *Return to 6.*

⓼ STRAD

from 73

"I have it," you say. "Reflect both the direction and the number. The direction showed forward 12, so we turn around and go back 21 steps."

The directions take you to a bush. Partially hidden is a much-loved, familiar-looking though slightly battered object.

"Watson, Watson! By the Lord Harry. It's the Strad! My missing violin!" You lift the precious Stradivarius eagerly and cradle it in your arms.

"What on earth is it doing here?" splutters Watson. "Who could have brought it here? And to what purpose?"

"Hmm. Someone has written 'Unlock' in chalk on the top of the case. But as you know I never lock it." Sure enough, it is not secured shut and opens easily. All's well. The most beautiful and best-loved of instruments looks unharmed. You examine it closely. And the bow is there. In the base of the case you see a small piece of sheet music. You bend down to retrieve it.

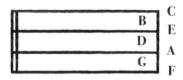

"Look at this, Watson – some kind of key? I wonder how the letters relate to musical notes? Pop the paper in your pocket, there's a good chap." You hand the note to Watson.

"Hold on," he says, looking at the reverse side of the sheet. "On the back there are four letters – MSAB."

You hold the instrument and move the bow above it.

"There are no strings, old man," Watson says.

"Not quite. I found one hanging from a tree branch a few hours ago."

You pull the string from your pocket and show it to Watson.

"This must be a string for the Stradivarius?" he asks.

"Indeed," you say, putting Strad and string away. "No time to waste." You hand the case to Watson and stride off towards the Waterloo Barracks.

▶ *Turn to 43.*

(53) SHERLOCK ON THE STAGE

from 66

"I keep thinking, Holmes," Watson begins, "that you are rather being set up as a musician this evening." He's laughing out loud now. "Are you ready for the stage?"

"Let's return to searching for this bottle, Watson," you retort.

"Although it might all be a little uncomfortable, no, Holmes?" he asks. "Given that Odon asked you for help and you refused."

You stop and turn to him. "What on earth are you talking about?" you ask.

"He wrote to you a few weeks ago asking for your attention on an urgent matter?" Watson responds. "You told me that the matter was beneath you and asked me to throw his letter away."

You had not forgotten. It was a drab letter full of rambling claims of a top-secret plot. You begin to wonder whether if you had helped him then . . . But there is no time for conjecture. You return to rifling through the bushes.

▶ *Turn to 44.*

(54) EMPTY GLASSES

from 68

You reach out for the third glass, but Watson gently touches your arm, pulling it down. He says nothing, but he doesn't need to. You know it can't be right.

You'd hoped the gesture might reveal something to you, but no luck.

A breeze rustles through the room, shaking the windows on their hinges, rattling each of the wine glasses so they clink gently against each other and the table.

"The nameless thing . . ." Watson whispers playfully. He is slurring his words a little. How many has he had? You help yourself to another, too, and return to the wine glasses.

▶ *Return to 68.*

QUEENS QUIESCENT

from 37, 71, 89

You stand side by side with Watson in the Chapel of St Peter ad Vincula, eyes scanning the historic surroundings for clues. You look up at the beautiful beams of the roof, examine the large windows behind the altar, the pews, piles of books. Nothing catches your eye . . .

"This, Holmes," Watson instructs you pedantically, "is the burial place not only of Anne Boleyn and Catherine Howard but also of Lady Jane Grey. In a recent renovation of the chapel a marble pavement was laid before the altar bearing their coats of arms. Shall we?"

You stride eagerly down the church and admire the pavement. On the altar you find a note:

> From A to Z I lead you a
> merry dance,
> Spelling out in five your
> way below.
> For the first, count shields
> before the holy table.
> And for the third, tell the
> tails within those shields.
>
> Be sure to flip

"A code for us to work out our next destination, old man. Could spelling out your way below be directing us to a book of some kind?" he says.

"Or spelling out in five means we've got to look for a five-letter word?" you say.

"I think we're being directed to look for a book," he says.

▶ *To follow Watson to look for a book, turn to 93.*

▶ *You plump for a five-letter word. Convert its letters to numbers using the code [A=1 . . . Z=26], take the first from the last letter and turn to that number.*

CRADLE TOWER

You are now close to the Tower's edge, and can almost hear the soothing lull of the Thames outside. Or is that in your mind? Watson is talking, you realize, and you tune in to the sound of his voice.

"John Gerard and John Arden," he says, "escaped this very tower on a rope stretched from Tower to Thames."

You consider the room. There is a mound of black fabric, its top attached to a rope with a hook. The rope runs across the ceiling through two pulleys and dangles in a far corner, with a small note attached.

You read it aloud: "The Sweet Thames runs softly, does it not? I wonder what the Thames will be thick with tomorrow? Will that be sweet? What will you be helpless to stop? What will you watch with horror? The clock is ticking. Can you find your way through the maze?"

"Find your way through the maze?" asks Watson. "Does he mean escape the Tower?"

You pull at the rope hanging in front of you, which lifts the black fabric off the floor revealing a maze, coiled in rope. 'Where to begin?' is chalked just below. You move close to puzzle your way through.

▶ *Go to the number corresponding to the correct entry.*

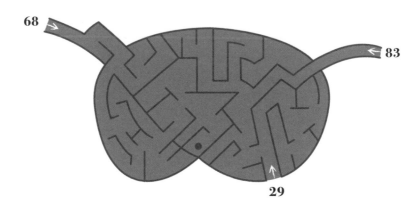

IN THE FRAME

You find you are stuck within the cage. So close, but unable to effect the rescue for which you have worked so hard. One misstep here or there was the difference between success and failure.

You look despairingly at Odon and Watson, now both pacing unhappily up and down within the enclosure. You are all in the frame for the attempted theft of the Crown Jewels, you see. Outside it sounds as if there is a great deal of bustle and movement. You can hear applause, and shouts of "God save the Queen!" The orchestra plays the national anthem. But then, just as you and Odon are rather miserably expecting to hear the beginning of his piece, the covering of the cage is brusquely lifted upwards, leaving you all exposed.

There are gasps and further shouts. You see Inspector Lestrade alongside a tall, thin monk.

"Andor!" Odon says.

"And here," Odon's brother declares dramatically, "we have the villains! I am sorry to report that my brother Odon has disgraced himself by becoming embroiled in a plot to steal the Crown Jewels. With the most unlikely pair of accomplices."

"Holmes? Dr Watson? I am amazed," gasps Lestrade.

"It is not true," Odon tries to say. "My brother Andor, who should be ashamed to be wearing his monk's habit, is the one plotting theft . . . theft of the riches of his own Abbey . . ."

"Professor Moriarty is his accomplice and attempting another great deception," Watson shouts in exasperation.

Andor merely holds his hands out, palms upwards, and looks at Lestrade. "Moriarty? Who on earth is that? I don't know him. These are the desperate claims of thieves who have been caught red-handed," he says.

"Entirely unbelievable," Lestrade says grimly to you, Watson and poor Odon. "You had better come along with us," he adds, ushering policemen into the enclosure to take you, all three, into custody.

▶ *Turn to 85.*

ST JOHN'S CHAPEL

from 76

Back at the White Tower, Watson leads the way up the stairs to the second storey.

On entering the chapel, you are both silenced; moved to stillness. No words can do justice to the beauty of the Chapel's domed vault, curved gallery and elegant Romanesque arches.

"The Normans may have had a martial bent, but they had something of an eye for beauty as well," Watson says rather too loudly. "Here, Holmes, we are taken right back to the time of William the Conqueror. This chapel has been standing for more than eight hundred years, since 1078."

But a certain Professor Moriarty has been busy much more recently, you note in the stronger morning light falling through the windows. Wherever you have been your redoubtable foe has been there first . . . you are merely following a path he has set through the Tower.

You are piecing together the puzzle, but there is still much that is troubling. Odon must be somewhere ahead of you in the sequence of rooms. There is a concert later this morning on the bridge to celebrate the Queen's longevity on the throne. She herself will be in attendance. Is she in danger?

"Someone with a much less-developed sense of the beautiful has been at work with a paintbrush," you say.

The doctor has seen it, too. "The work of nothing less than a vandal!" he shouts angrily.

"Come, time is moving on. Let us concentrate on decoding the message," you say, "and determining our next destination."

What does the clock indicate? And why has the column furthest to the right been clumsily painted over?

▶ *Work out the next number in the sequence and turn to that paragraph.*

BOLTS AND KEYS

from 90

"It is 59!" you exclaim triumphantly.

Watson looks a little perplexed. "What does 59 mean, though, Holmes?" he asks. "Is there a 59 on the map?"

Together you inspect the map closely, but there is no 59 to be seen. You experience a rare frisson of doubt. You move to return to the sketch and your position, which is hard to find with so many bolts and beams in the way.

You look down at the floor and note something. "Look here, Watson," you say. "I do believe each of these bolts is numbered?"

Watson inspects the floor at his feet and agrees.

"Perhaps," you say, "we are looking for bolt 59?"

You begin your search. The numbers appear to be random, so it's no easy task. The morning sun beats down against your neck, reminding you with each beam that you are edging closer and closer to 11.30 a.m. Your chance of foiling Moriarty's plans is slipping away.

"Here!" Watson calls. He is brandishing an old and tarnished brass key.

"This was tied to bolt 59! Our musical friend has saved us!" he exclaims. "We just need to make our way to where Odon is trapped, and we'll be able to release him."

You let this new information sink in. After all of Moriarty's tricks and jibes, one key tied to a bolt feels far too simple.

"Show a leg, Holmes," Watson calls as he makes his way towards the large covered box. "I think we should start here."

You leave your reservations behind and follow him.

▶ *Turn to 8.*

THE BLOODY TOWER

Watson climbs slowly, almost mournfully, up the winding stairs.

"Must have a look at the first floor," he says, so quietly you can barely hear him. Following him up the steeply winding stairs you rest your hand on the cool stones of the old, old walls, a place of such suffering. Trapped within the Tower, you think . . . you yourself have been clearly targeted for some test or game . . . However, you are increasingly intrigued. What could the note outside the Tower mean?

You are standing behind Watson in the upstairs chamber as he announces: "The Bloody Tower is where the young princes Edward V and his brother Richard supposedly disappeared in 1483 . . . the murder of the young innocents."

A message has been scrawled on the walls. Clearly some letters are missing, presumably indicating where you should go next.

▶ *Make a word from the missing letters and find your next destination on the map, then turn to the number indicated there.*

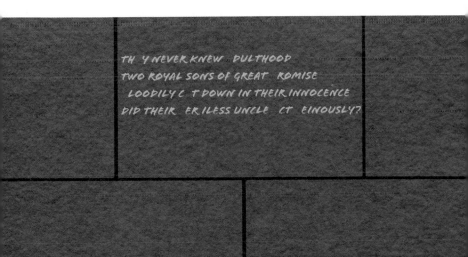

TH Y NEVER KNEW DULTHOOD
TWO ROYAL SONS OF GREAT ROMISE
LOODILY C T DOWN IN THEIR INNOCENCE
DID THEIR ER ILESS UNCLE CT EINOUSLY?

EMBARRASSED

from 91

"Hello? Holmes? Dr Watson?"

At last. You have been here for hours.

A familiar voice. The last notes of your latest attempt at one of Mendelssohn's lieder are just fading away. The all-too-familiar figure of Inspector Lestrade appears in the Well Tower doorway.

"Nero fiddled while Rome burned! What on earth are you doing, Holmes? When your country needed you, your queen at risk?"

You are embarrassed and remain silent.

"Inspector! What happened?" Watson is all eagerness.

"All is well, doctor. The warning you hung from the window was seen by a bobby on the beat and we managed to prevent any major difficulties on the Bridge. Your friend Odon von Mihalovic was found tied up with the Crown Jewels, no less, in a cage on the bridge. He is safe and free of suspicion. A notorious figure is in custody, and his plot in ruins." He looks at you.

"Professor Moriarty," you say.

"Of course, but he got the better of you. There was no time to come to rescue you both until now."

Watson is shivering while Lestrade continues: "Your sacrifice of your shirt and the discomfort you suffered as a result were well worth it. Her Majesty was informed of your actions and is inviting you, Watson, to tea at the Palace. So let's get everyone home. Come along Sherlock. Don't forget your violin."

THE END

The Evening Gazette

23 September 1896

PLOT FOILED ON TOWER BRIDGE, NOTORIOUS VILLAIN IN CUSTODY

ATTEMPT TO STEAL CROWN JEWELS FAILS; HER MAJESTY 'DELIGHTED' AS DR WATSON SAVES THE DAY

Celebrated sleuth Sherlock Holmes met his match today when he was outwitted by notorious villain Professor James Moriarty – whom many had assumed dead after the events at the Reichenbach Falls in '91. Holmes defeated Moriarty on that occasion but now seems to have lost his vim and vigour. Reports indicate that, trapped by Moriarty in the Tower, he simply gave up on finding a way to prevent not only the theft of the Crown Jewels but also the framing of esteemed composer Odon von Mihalovic, whose performance before the queen was almost cancelled. The detective was found playing his violin – like Nero, who fiddled while Rome burned.

If not for the brave and clever intervention of Dr Watson, who hung his shirt out a window to send a message warning of the plot and pleading for rescue, Moriarty's plan would have succeeded – with Otto von Mihalovic behind bars. Dr Watson's warning was seen by Constable James Nelson, who was on the beat and witnessed a flapping apparition at a small window. "I thought it was a ghost," he said. The wise doctor has been invited to meet the Queen.

(Continued on page 3)

TRAPPED BY THE WORLD'S MOST SECURE LOCK?

Composer-turned-jewel thief Odon von Mihalovic was held in a cage on Tower Bridge using what experts claim is the most secure lock in the world. There is only one key in existence for this lock, said to have been made in the Tower during the reign of King Henry VIII. Thankfully, Brother Andor took the correct course of action, using the lock to contain the criminal until Scotland Yard could apprehend him.

HALLÉ ORCHESTRA SHINES, NERUDA MAGNIFICENT

The foiling of the audacious plot allowed the planned performance of Odon von Mihalovic's orchestral piece 'Sweet Thames Run Softly' to be performed to a select audience that included Her Majesty Queen Victoria to celebrate her becoming Britain's longest-ruling monarch. The Hallé Orchestra from Manchester was magnificent, with a haunting solo performed by leading violinist Wilhelmine Norman Neruda that was highly praised. Of Holmes's inability to escape the Tower of London, the soloist said, "I am sad that Mr Holmes was not present as I hoped he would be able to enjoy both my efforts and my performance, but it was not to be."

CONCERNS DISMISSED, SAYS LANDLADY OF VEILED LODGER

A Brixton landlady, a certain Mrs Merrilow, repeated her "serious concerns" to local police about her veiled lodger, who she heard crying "Murder, murder!" at night.

(62) THE STAIRWELL

from 30

You take the left fork.

The howls and groans of the tunnel continue to chase you. You know rationally there is nothing there, but you keep moving faster and faster. The concert edges closer and closer.

After a few minutes the nature of the tunnel changes. You are no longer in walls made of packed dirt but now in a path constructed of metal. You look around. You are getting closer to it, whatever it is.

Suddenly you are at the end of the path, and at the bottom of a staircase. You have wholly lost your sense of direction, and have no clue as to whether you'll emerge in the middle of the Thames, or on the opposite bank. You desperately hope you won't find yourself in one of London's infamous sewers.

You look at Watson and he nods. No need for words here. You make a move towards the staircase. As you climb onto the first step, something knocks against your leg. It is a small coil of paper: on one side there are musical staves. The paper looks like it has been torn out of a composer's notebook. On the other side is a small sketch of the Tower of London. The perspective is odd, high up, and not one you've seen before. You show the sketch to Watson.

"Do you think this means we're headed back into the Tower?" Watson asks.

"I do hope not," you respond, "but there is only one way to find out." You pocket the sketch and begin to climb.

► *Turn to 90.*

TRIANGULATION

from 38

Watson is standing near a geometric image, which has been scratched into the wall. Below it is a short message: *Where next? How many triangles?*

You consider the image. The crossed lines make triangles of all kinds and sizes, and triangles combine to make larger triangles again. You begin to count, but your thoughts feel a little scrambled.

You concentrate and still your mind. You can't let Moriarty in – you can't let him win. You need to focus. You stand completely still, eyes trained on the wall, and an answer begins to appear to you.

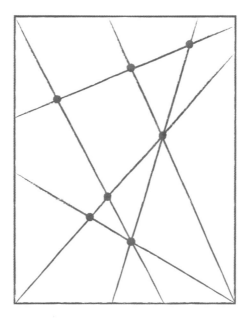

WHERE NEXT? HOW MANY TRIANGLES?

▶ *Once you have your answer, turn to the passage with the same number.*

INCORRECT TUNNEL

from 30

You follow Watson's instincts and head down the right fork. After a few metres, the path loops around and you begin to head back the way you have come, towards the Tower. You stop.

"This can't be right?" you ask.

Watson shakes his head.

"I believe I may have been wrong, Holmes," Watson says. He appears to have calmed down a little now. Watson carries on chuntering, but you are hardly listening. The minutes are slipping away and you're already on your way back towards the fork in the path.

▶ *Return to 30.*

POSTERN GATE

from 20

Holding the map, Watson takes the lead on the way to the Postern Gate. It is a ruined gateway, which must have allowed important guests landing from the river to access the Royal Palace at the Tower. But there is no evidence of your note-writing guide having left a message here. You must have interpreted something wrongly.

"Nothing to see here," Watson declares. You follow him back to Traitors' Gate.

▶ *Return to 20.*

You move towards the sound of the notes, and emerge in a small clearing. Watson is initially petulant, keen to keep moving, but his resistance lasts a matter of moments and soon he is back to regaling you with tales of the Tower. You tune in.

"In fact," he is saying, "although the Tower is primarily associated with crime and bloodshed, it has a rich history of art and culture, too." You nod, but you are distracted when you catch sight of something in the bushes to your right.

"During the reign of Henry VIII this included royal trumpeter John Blanke," he continues. You pause a moment to listen. "Blanke is thought to have travelled over to England with Katherine of Aragon. He played for many years in the royal court. Amazingly, he argued with the king that his wages should be doubled – to no less than 16 pence a day – and succeeded."

Watson finishes with a flourish. You do wonder where he found the time to prepare in such detail.

You move towards the bushes, and there, entwined with the leaves and branches, is another scroll of paper. You pull it out and hand it to Watson. Unravelled, the scroll shows a single bar of music, this time with the word 'Love' above it. You slide it into your pocket. You have a sense this won't be the last time you consider this short piece of music. Together you move out of the clearing.

▶ *Turn to 53.*

HEADQUARTERS OF THE FUSILIERS

from 43

"Flagstone 3. . . Which indicates the letters 'H', 'Q'. Where does that lead us on the map, Watson?"

"Aha! Fusiliers! The Headquarters of the Fusiliers!" Watson exclaims, with perhaps a little too much glee, as you move to stand outside the wooden doors. He launches off: "About 50 years ago a fire destroyed the depot that once stood here, and this building was put up instead. I'm sure there's a story of the wronged souls of the Tower setting a fire in revenge, but I can't seem to quite remember it . . ."

"Hmm," you respond, making a move towards a wall, just to your right, where you can see something painted onto the brickwork. The "hmm" seems to have been enough, and Watson quietly follows you.

The courtyard is notably silent. Yet another building that should be full of people appears to be deserted. This and the increasing scale of Moriarty's puzzles is giving you pause. He's put a little more effort into this than you first anticipated.

Watson is reviewing the puzzle on the wall and you go to join him. There is a short message and then some images of archery targets. Arrows are painted to have landed on the numbers 6 and 23 and the letters 'F', 'M' and 'T'. Targets coloured red, blue and green remain.

Watson reads the message out loud: "With one final arrow, get as close as you can to 100. But if you go over, you'll lose everything. Spin, spin Sherlock. A colour could represent any of its numbers, and until it has landed there is no way to find out."

"Spin, spin?" Watson asks. You are already lifting the code wheel out of your pocket.

▶ *To shoot your arrow at the red target, turn to 48.*

▶ *To shoot your arrow at the blue target, turn to 69.*

▶ *To shoot your arrow at the green target, turn to 94.*

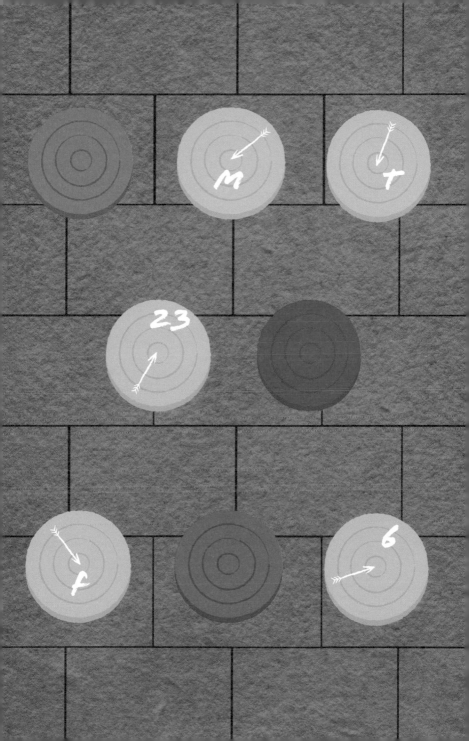

YEOMAN WARDERS' CLUB

You push open the door of the Yeoman Warders' Club to reveal a small but perfectly formed pub.

"One of the most exclusive pubs in the world," Watson remarks. "Open only to the Yeoman Warders and their guests."

"Where are they all?" You wonder aloud. How has Moriarty cleared the Tower? What connection does he have with the Beefeaters? What does their absence mean for tomorrow's events?

Watson pours himself a pint of bitter, sips it and continues. "Many say it is more than just the Warders who live here, of course. Endless ghosts are rumoured to wander the flagstones. The guards even have their own spirit, known only as the 'nameless thing'." He smiles and chuckles, to whom you are not sure. Himself maybe?

You pour yourself a drink and pull out your watch to check the time . . . 5.02 p.m. As you do, Watson stumbles backwards, knocking your watch out of your hand so it falls into a glass of gin and hits the bottom heavily. The hands swirl round and come to a stop, Your timepiece is ruined.

Watson appears unruffled. "Come and look at this," he says, beckoning you over. You follow begrudgingly. He is standing in front of several glasses of wine. More drinks, you wonder?

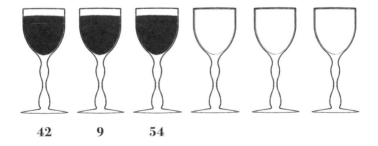

42   9   54

Watson reads out the puzzle written just below: "Three full glasses of wine are followed by three empty glasses. By only moving one glass of wine, rearrange the pattern so each full glass is followed by an empty one. Which glass?"

Below each full glass of wine is a small number.

You let the alcohol and puzzle swill in your mind and an answer begins to materialize.

▶ *Turn to the passage that corresponds to the glass you want to move.*

⑥⑨ TARGETING BLUE

from 67

"I think it has to be blue," Watson begins. He spins the code wheel in front of you. "Look, all these numbers are so low, there's no chance we'd go over. The colour of the Royal Fusiliers is blue, too, Holmes, so it's a perfect fit!"

It's very unlike Watson to be quite so imprecise you think. Perhaps those 2? 3? 4? pints of bitter had more of an effect than you realized . . .

"No chance?" you ask.

Watson notes your tone, but says nothing.

"Not quite no chance," he mutters.

You nod and the two of you return to the puzzle at hand.

▶ *Return to 67.*

TOWER VIEW

You reach a break in the path and, as expected, find the number 70 painted on the ground in the same paint.

"This is the spot," you tell Watson. "And here is confirmation." What's more, your sharp eyes have spotted a note stuck into a crevice in the ancient wall. Taking and unfolding the paper you read the handwritten message and take in the view, with Watson at your side.

You admire the September afternoon light once more. The sun touches the sweet Thames while the river's tidal waters move a boat and several barges. A light wind ruffles the trees on the bank.

"Such a peaceful scene," murmurs Watson, "yet there has been so much suffering here; so many accused of plotting and treachery. Dragged, begging for mercy, into the Tower of London. Often through the water-gate on the river. The great Queen Elizabeth, when a princess . . ."

"'Yes, yes." You clear your throat. "Now, to work. If our mystery letter-writer is so keen for us to stand in a particular place, there is in all likelihood something particular about the view from it."

What could be the meaning of providing drawings of several common items in the note? You scan the scene, and ponder.

And the wording? Where can that be leading?

Gather together. What might that suggest? Find the right position. Clearly you have a code of some kind.

"I think it's fair to say," you announce, "that we are looking for a way to convert these images into a word. There are seven images, so a seven-letter word. And this word will tell us where to go next."

▶ *Turn to the passage that corresponds to the first letter in the word.*

Gather together, then find
the right position.
I'll be seeing you soon, Holmes.

PROTHALAMION . . . PUZZLED IN ST PETER'S

I can't make sense of it, you think. You're beginning to feel a little weary. Perhaps you need a breather. You walk with Watson to the back of the church, where you stand looking out. Your mind drifts back to the scene on the riverside, the sparkling water, the Bridge and the notice of the concert. *Sweet Thames*. What is that line that old Odon quoted in the title of his piece, you wonder . . .?

"Spenser, old man," murmurs Watson. Did you say the question out loud? "A wedding poem called 'Prothalamion'. 'Sweet Thames run softly, till I end my song'."

"Yes, yes. But how can we find where to go next?"

The doctor is silent.

"Watson?"

"Eh? Holmes, my apologies, I was only thinking that by my reckoning it is three centuries exactly since Edmund Spenser wrote those lines in 1596. Here we are again near the end of a different century in '96 and our Queen is celebrating becoming this country's longest-reigning monarch . . ."

"Yes, Watson." You shake your head. But he has given you a nudge.

"I think we should try counting again," you say.

▶ *Return to 55.*

INSIDE THE CONSTABLE TOWER DRINKS CABINET

You wonder whether a clue might be hidden in the drinks cabinet.

"It's the kind of place a fellow might hide something behind a bottle or inside an empty ice bucket or something," Watson says, curiously picking up once again on your unspoken thoughts.

Sure enough, behind a bottle of Pattison's Royal Gordon you find a letter typed on the lightest typing paper folded into a long, thin oblong.

September 15, 1896

Dear Sir Daniel

To confirm: you have agreed to guarantee that all of the Tower's guards, other personnel and residents will be absent on the 22nd of this month for a period of forty-eight hours. I enclose the amount of one hundred pounds, as agreed. But mark my words: if you don't do as arranged, I will release the information as discussed.

Yours most gratefully,
Jaime A Jority

"Well, that explains where everyone is," Watson says. "Absolutely shocking that the Constable of the Tower should abandon post."

"This is getting quite serious, Watson," you add. "Corruption in high places."

"Who is this Jority? What a strange first name. Is he a Finn or something?"

"An anagram, Watson, for a much more familiar name. I think you'll be able to work it out."

▶ *To investigate the pile of papers, turn to 86.*

▶ *To examine the desk, turn to 39.*

▶ *To sit at the table, turn to 79.*

FOLLOW THE MUSIC

The music seems to be coming from a tree. How is that possible? You stride eagerly across the open space. High up, at the limit of your reach, you see a small box hidden in the joint between trunk and branch. The tune is most certainly being emitted by this machine. You are just able to get it down.

"A musical box, Watson, and attached to it by a string a small paper bearing a message . . ."

"Reflected words, I would say, yes?" offers Watson.

"Hmm, 'Music feeds the Soul'." You flip it over. "Anything on the back? Ah, yes."

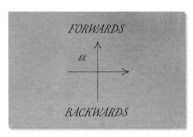

"We're being directed to look somewhere perhaps?," asks Watson. "Maybe the reflected words indicate we should change direction and go 12 steps back?"

"No, Watson, reflect again: both the direction and the number."

▶ *Reflect twice: direction and number. Turn to that passage.*

ANOTHER STRING

from 36

You walk towards the sound of the note. As you venture away from the Constable Tower you begin to lose access to any artificial light and Watson has to take his matches from his pocket to attempt to light your way.

As he lights the fourth match you notice something stuck between two flagstones just under your step.

The match burns to its base and Watson drops it, grimacing, onto the floor. "Light another," you call out. "There seems to be a small wooden box underfoot."

You retrieve the box and open it delicately to reveal a small rolled-up piece of paper – another piece of music. This one has the word 'For' written across the top. You mentally store the note and then slide the scrap of paper into your pocket.

"What on earth do you think these notes are for?" Watson asks.

You shake your head and respond, "I don't know. I feel as though they are trying to tell me something, but I'm not sure what yet."

Watson picks up the violin case and you return to the path.

► *Turn to 49.*

You realize Watson has been speaking and pull yourself back to the room.

"Come over and see this." Watson is watching the Bridge, and what appears to be a crane depositing on its main walkway a large box that seems to be covered in dark material. "It must be for the concert," he says, turning away.

You look a little while longer. Something doesn't feel right. The concert was all set up this morning. You saw it. What is this oblong box? Why is it being added now?

"What an odd note from Moriarty," Watson comments. "Why do you think he keeps referencing Odon's piece?"

You receive Watson's words. You hadn't quite thought of it that way, but he's right. Moriarty's messages do reference Odon's composition. How odd.

"Where next?" Watson asks. "Was there a puzzle?"

"Yes," you respond, and read it aloud.

"Here in the attic is a pile of 60 gems: 20 green emeralds, 20 clear diamonds, 20 red rubies. They are all cut identically; impossible to distinguish by touch. In a moment the light will go out. What is the minimum number of gems you will need to take downstairs with you to be sure you are holding three gems of the same type?"

Watson smiles at you. "Let's just take all 60, Holmes?" he chuckles.

"I think we should be careful what we put in our pockets, old chap," you respond. "I have a feeling that it'll come to be far more important than we understand yet."

You set about solving the puzzle.

▶ *Use your answer and the map to find your next location.*

from 45, 81

You have a sense that you have let Odon down, but you are careful to remind yourself that rushing is of no benefit. A cool head is what is needed.

Watson is hot on your heels.

"Anything useful to report, Watson?" you ask.

He manages a weak smile, as though grateful for the distraction. "Remarkable tale, actually, though how useful I'm not sure . . . this tower is named after Robert Devereux, Earl of Essex, a great nobleman imprisoned here after attempting a rebellion and thus falling out with Elizabeth I. He had a signet ring from Elizabeth who told him that if he ever returned it to her he would be forgiven, whatever he had done. He tried to do just that, dropping it from the tower to a passing pageboy with instructions to give it to the Queen, but the boy instead gave it to Devereux's great enemy Lady Nottingham. She kept it."

"Interesting, indeed," you nod, your eyes busily scanning the chamber for clues. You see chalked on the wall:

LOOK ALERT, SHERLOCK
HOLMES. LET'S REMEMBER,
YOUR ALLIES ARE NOT
ALWAYS YOUR FRIENDS.
SPINUM
A, L

You muse over the inscription. "It appears that our enemy may also be familiar with the tale you just recounted, Watson."

"What does the message mean, Holmes? How does it lead us to our next destination?"

▶ *Decode the message. The map might come in handy.*

INSPECTING THE COLDHARBOUR RUINS

"Hold on Watson, let us just have a further look here. Around this side, for instance . . ."

You crouch down low, inspecting the ground-level ruins. Watson is coming up behind you to help when he exclaims: "Here we are!"

Looking up, you see a message chalked carefully on the upper stones of the tower ruin.

▶ *Decode the message then turn to the number indicated by the third letter.*

PIECE B

"If you hold it at this angle surely this is the missing piece?" Watson asks, rather weakly.

"I can't see how that's the correct answer, Watson," you say. 'We must try again."

▶ *Return to 50.*

AMBUSHED BY . . .

Watson is eagerly eyeing the food laid out on the central table.

"Maybe a bite to eat and a glass of something restorative before we go any further, Holmes?"

Feeling more than a little weary, you sit in one of the armchairs near the central table.

"Rather fine port," says Watson, pouring a second glass for himself and one for you. "And truly excellent sandwiches. Roast beef and horseradish."

You join him. They are rather good. He offers you a piece of Victoria sponge. "I am not a child, Watson. I would prefer a piece of that rather excellent-looking fruit cake."

Watson sits in the other easy chair and, within a few moments, is breathing deeply. His need for sleep is ridiculous. The windows are dark, and you wonder vaguely what the time is now. You hear what could be a raven flapping its wings outside the window.

You are happy to spend a few peaceful moments thinking through the case. But your eyes droop. A thought pops into your head that you should really have kept count of the number of steps you went up and down in the many, many towers. Again, your eyes droop, and darkness seems to flow in through the windows from the London night. You have been ambushed by . . . sleep.

▶ *Turn to 41.*

ST THOMAS'S TOWER

from 20

Together, you follow the cannonballs' directions and find yourself at St Thomas's Tower. You can feel the fortress growing around you as you take these first steps inside; the imposing walls cast long shadows at your feet. As you watch them you notice something peculiar. You beckon Watson over.

"Can you see these differently coloured stones?" You point to a line of reddish pebbles laid in the gravel.

"Perhaps we should follow them?" Watson responds. You are already halfway along the path.

The reddish stones fittingly deposit you at the Bloody Tower. You are at the edge of the Tower of London now. You note a rusty old portcullis hanging in the archway. This gate is defunct now, you imagine.

Watson is poring over the brickwork in the wall, stroking his moustache and gently whispering the word 'peculiar'. You go to join him. Several bricks are set back slightly. Some have a small, etched image: a moon, a flame, the sun, a lightning bolt; three have numbers: 82, 46, 23.

A message is also scratched into the brickwork. It reads:

A crowned fire
Remarks at the moonlight
Beguiled under the sun
Loses the lightning

And below, in a different hand: *The Gods above and beasts below are watching. What direction are you headed? Let's begin, Sherlock.* Begin is underlined.

Watson looks stumped. You muse aloud: "I would posit that we need to select a brick to finish this pattern?"

Watson nods. "But what can this message mean?" The words and bricks meld in your mind as the solution becomes clear.

▶ *Turn to the passage corresponding to the brick you choose.*

(81) A WOBBLING FLAGSTONE

from 45

You identify the stone that you tripped over and give it a quick kick. The flagstone shifts under the impulse, and you lift it up.

Underneath is a small scrap of parchment. It looks impossibly old, almost as though it might turn to dust at the lightest touch. A message is written on the front. You read it aloud:

"Where water is raised, descend. Freedom lies below."

Watson is watching you. "What can that mean, Holmes?"

"I'm not sure," you respond, moving the flagstone to cover the message once more.

You get up to move on, but the words have lodged themselves in your mind. 'Water above, freedom below'. How will you escape?

▶ *Turn to 76.*

BRICK 82

"It is 82!" Watson exclaims. His moustache trembles a little with excitement. He launches into his logic: "See this line here," he says, stabbing his finger on the scratched message. "The gods above!" He looks at you, and continues: "This number 82 is at the very top, you see, above all the others." He looks extremely elated.

You can't quite bring yourself to point out the second half of the phrase. You hope he'll get there himself and, as expected . . . "Ah, but the beasts below. That doesn't quite work, does it?"

He looks at you apologetically. You shake your head.

The two of you return to the puzzle. Watson appears very slightly dejected, but something in the direction of his thinking has given you an idea.

▶ *Return to 80.*

TWISTED ROPE

Watson taps his finger on 83 and then traces it through the maze. He gets stuck and then sighs.

"That can't be right," he urges. "I just felt like we were getting to the centre of it all – Moriarty's plot, why we're here – and now we're stumped by this!" Watson's words sink into the room and reveal something.

You return to the maze to consider it one last time.

▶ *Turn to 56.*

"GOD SAVE THE QUEEN"

from 92

Odon is hurried to the front of the audience seating to shake hands with the conductor Edward Elgar, and to find the space reserved for him. You and Watson look without success for a place and opt to stand at the back. The orchestra is warming up.

"Holmes, what a haunting tone!"

Looking across, you see Wilhelmine Norman-Neruda, one of your favourite violinists. She catches your eye as she plays a note. The sun comes briefly from behind a cloud and touches her reddish-gold hair. It triggers a memory of seeing a flash of hair in the Tower during the night. And you wonder, is there something familiar about the note she plays?

Was she involved in the plot in some way? Who left the strings and bars of music for you in the Tower?

Soon everyone is standing as the orchestra launches into 'God Save the Queen' and Her Majesty is ushered in to take a seat at the very front. The sun comes out fully as the musicians begin 'Sweet Thames Run Softly' and you close your eyes.

▶ *Turn to 27.*

DESPAIRING

from 57

Looking gloomily around the police cell in which you are being held with Watson, it feels like it has been the longest of days. But you realize it is only late afternoon on the day of the cancelled concert. You are still reviewing the various steps you took in trying to solve the challenge, determined to work out where you went wrong. You are calm, but frustrated . . . And, today, despairing. Watson sits behind you, his head in his hands. They have taken away the Stradivarius to the evidence room.

The cell door opens. As if things could get any worse . . . Enter Mycroft, wearing a smug grin.

"My dear brother, Sherlock, this has not ended very well for you and the good doctor, has it? You must be more careful. I am working on your release, but it is proving harder than I imagined. The Palace, in particular, is proving very difficult to appease."

Watson speaks up: "What of Odon?"

"I am afraid that his days of freedom appear to be over. The most we can arrange will be for him to be incarcerated in relative comfort and perhaps supplied with manuscript paper to continue his rather excellent compositions."

"Brother Andor?"

"He is giving interviews to the newspapers, emphasizing his commitment to Pannonhalma Abbey and concern for his brother. Anything to say in your defence, Sherlock? Any way I can be of assistance?"

You will not ask him for help.

"Well, well, well. You have been rather stupid. However you were involved in this scheme, you two, you have demonstrably failed. I will be on my way. Perhaps you would like to read this afternoon's *Gazette*? Mummy sends her commiserations. She wanted to visit, but I had the most terrible time getting permission from the tiresome Lestrade to come myself. So long, chum."

THE END

The Evening Gazette

23 September 1896

PLOT FOILED ON TOWER BRIDGE, CELEBRATED COMPOSER AND DETECTIVE IN CUSTODY

CROWN JEWELS HEIST FAILS; MUSICAL GREAT ODON VON MIHALOVIC AND BAKER STREET'S FINEST SHERLOCK HOLMES SHAMED

Hungarian composer Odon von Mihalovic and detective Sherlock Holmes are in detention with Scotland Yard this evening, having been caught red-handed trying to steal the Crown Jewels. Their associate Dr John Watson was also apprehended. The plot was revealed by Benedictine monk Andor von Mihalovic, who said he was shocked by the revelation that his brother was a criminal.

The disgraced detective's brother Mycroft Holmes said, "Sherlock has been made to look very foolish, but perhaps there is more that needs to be uncovered before we can draw definitive conclusions about the case." However, given the overwhelming evidence against him, it is difficult to conceive of any fate for Sherlock that isn't a long custodial sentence. (Continued on page 3)

(Continued on page 3)

WORLD'S MOST SECURE LOCK?

The villains were held in a cage on Tower Bridge using what experts claim is the most secure lock in the world. There is only one key in existence for this lock, said to have been made in the Tower during the reign of King Henry VIII. Thankfully, Andor von Mihalovic took the correct course of action, using the lock to contain the criminals until Scotland Yard could apprehend them.

'SWEET THAMES' DOES NOT RUN

The uncovering of the plot meant the cancellation of the planned performance of disgraced composer Odon von Mihalovic's orchestral piece 'Sweet Thames Run Softly', which was to have been performed to a select audience including Her Majesty Queen Victoria to celebrate her becoming Britain's longest-ruling monarch. Soloist Wilhelmine Norman Neruda was not available for comment.

BROTHER FOILS PLOT

The hero of the day, Andor von Mihalovic, was humble when questioned about his extraordinary bravery in the face of this scheme of treachery and treason. It stands to reason that he will now soon become Abbot of Pannonhalma Abbey. Recovering at The Ritz Hotel after his daring rescue of the nation's treasure, he said: "In my hands, the future of the Abbey will be safe."

ALLEGATIONS OF VAMPIRE ACTIVITY PLAYED DOWN

Claims of vampire activity in Sussex have been played down by the local constabulary. A local man involved in the case, Mr Robert Ferguson, declined to comment.

A PILE OF PAPERS AT THE CONSTABLE TOWER

"I wonder what we can find in this pile of papers?" You ask. "I must say, the Constable's office efficiency leaves something to be desired."

The heap of papers looks to have been shuffled across the floor and is partially collapsing. Watson lifts a paper from the top.

"Underneath, Holmes, look, is a report from a Hungarian newspaper with pictures of books and musical instruments and sheet music in a grand setting . . ."

". . . And here on top," you say, taking the paper from Watson, "a sheet from a translation agency."

> Word to Word Translations
> August 1, 1896
> Dear Sir,
> The paragraphs you wanted translated from Hungarian read:
>
> News from the magnificent Pannonhalma Abbey, where Brother Andor von Mihalovic is poised to be named Abbot on September 23. He will have complete freedom to reorganize and streamline the library's holdings, which date back over 1,000 years. His appointment is being seen as safeguarding the future of the library.

"We read about that chap outside St Peter's," Watson says. "He's Odon's brother. And September 23 is tomorrow, old man." He is looking through the rest of the papers. "Nothing else here of any interest, Holmes. It's all materials to do with delivery of supplies to the Tower."

► *To look in the drinks cabinet, turn to 72.*

► *To examine the desk, turn to 39.*

► *To sit at the table, turn to 79.*

LOST FOR WORDS IN THE SALT TOWER

You both stand there, at something of a loss.

"He writes 'spell it out' . . ." you say, "though CGMBD spells . . ."

"Nothing," Watson says.

You wander over to the window, your feet crunching on the salt grains Watson spilled when he opened the note so clumsily. Looking out, the river is visible, glistening in the early autumn afternoon. You look across at Tower Bridge. Tomorrow's event is taking place there, and whatever plot Moriarty has hatched must surely involve it. Yet you are here in the Tower, going round and round.

Your focus shifts. On the window glass before your nose, written with a finger in the dust, you see the word 'TRAPPED'. He is making fun of you.

"Could it be," ventures Watson, "simply that the first letter indicates the chimneybreast?"

You shrug. "We can but try . . ."

He hurries across to the chimney.

▶ *Turn to 51.*

BYWARD TOWER

"Yes, I agree with you," says Watson. "It must be the first piece, which leads us to 88." He looks it up on the map. Byward Tower. It is just a short walk from the inner to the outer wall, from the Bell Tower to the Byward.

You walk into the tower and glance around quickly. You are momentarily stunned. Painted on the wall, on either side of the large fireplace is a beautiful, ornate mural. It shows Saint Michael, and a number of other figures, standing on a long stretch of green grass. Michael is wearing blue robes and a gold crown. His red wings reach far above his head and then down to his waist.

"It's striking, isn't it Holmes," says Watson, turning to you. You nod.

Below the image, someone has written three lines:

To follow the ground, go to Devereux.
To follow the robes, go to the North Bastion.
To follow the wings, go to the Broad Arrow Tower.

You gesture towards the sentences. "What can these mean?" you ask Watson, who is scrabbling around on the floor.

He stands up, brandishing a coil of paper.

"This, Holmes, I believe is the puzzle."

You read it over his shoulder.

In time, there will be a day of judgement. It will be taken. All will gather together to determine what is to become of him, the traitor. Strapped to the wheel. At the **start**, Some truths will be revealed and **with** them **a** lie will be hidden, and in the midst of it you will be caught. **Turned** over. Trapped. Sixes and sevens. Unable to stop, unable to act, unable to make change. You will have no **places**. After the day of judgement, nothing will be **left**. There will be one new ruler, and I will have won.

"Do you think it describes the scene ahead?" Watson asks, "or us?"

"Both, perhaps," you respond. "But more importantly, the message contains a puzzle."

▶ *Use the map to find your next location.*

from 14

(89) A BENEDICTINE CONNECTION

You make your way into St Peter ad Vincula.

"Did you know, Holmes, this is actually a parish church for the Tower of London?"

You roll your eyes.

Next Watson points out a noticeboard at the entry and begins reading out its contents. Service times, confirmation class, an offer of organ tuition. One clipping particularly catches his eye. He reads it aloud: "HUNGARIAN ABBOT-IN-WAITING TO ATTEND CELEBRATION CONCERT. Many foreign dignitaries and guests will be attending the celebrations on Tower Bridge on 23 September in honour of Queen Victoria becoming Britain's longest-reigning monarch. Among them will be the composer's brother, Brother Andor, soon to be named as Abbot of the historic Pannonhalma Abbey in Hungary, home to a magnificent musical library."

▶ *Turn to 55.*

TOWER BRIDGE

from 62

You emerge at the top of one of the towers on Tower Bridge.

"My goodness, quite a climb," Watson says, breathing heavily. He leans against you briefly.

Remarkable, you think, that those Tudor tunnels were forgotten for hundreds of years. And even more so that they could have been extended to run halfway beneath the river to the towers of the Bridge.

"A fine September morning," the doctor says, "It's a good thing we both have a head for heights . . ."

You look sharply down and around in all directions, still seeking Odon. The concert is scheduled for 11.30 a.m. Moriarty's plot must be set to reach its climax then, about four hours from now.

You have the precious Stradivarius now. And those puzzling notes. What role could there be in all this for that?

Watson moves away from you. "Look, Holmes, what could that be?"

It's no clearer what the oblong structure is from here than it was when we saw it being lowered onto the bridge before.

"Come along. Our friend Odon could be down there."

You place your hand on Watson's arm. "Things are falling into place," you murmur. Your hand reaches into your pocket.

Looking down at the Tower of London complex on the bank, your eye catches on the portcullis in the gateway. You shiver.

"We must be in the correct spot here, Watson, because this view matches exactly the one in the sketch we found earlier."

Or not exactly. There are certain differences. And see here. Scratched on the wall in chalk is the message: 'Look closely within and on the Tower walls. Initially take note. Spin your way and bring them together.'

You hold the sketch in your left hand and take in the view.

▶ *Decode Moriarty's latest instructions to find*
your next destination on the map.

AT A LOSS IN THE WELL TOWER

"I suggest those messages about freedom and water were linked to some plot for escape during the Tower's long history," you say.

"Fascinating," notes Watson. "Yes."

"Now to work." You continue your search of the Well Tower. On. And on. And on. But for all your clarity of vision and perspicacity and determination, you're unable to find anything beyond a single stick of charcoal. You both sit, disconsolate, on the floor.

"We must do something, Holmes. We cannot just wait here for inspiration. Time is short and we both know some shocking event or revelation is planned for the concert on Tower Bridge."

"Watson, I am at a loss." You are amazed to hear yourself say it. The silence sits heavily on you both. Then your eyes fall on the Stradivarius case. You wonder . . . There must be a reason why the strings were removed and returned to you. "Give me the strings from your pocket, please." You set to restringing the violin. Could a tune from the old girl attract help?

When you look across, you see that Watson is disrobing.

You ignore him, concentrate on the strings and tune your beloved Strad.

Now he is writing a message with the charcoal on his shirt and hanging it out of the window above the wharf.

"What on earth, dear fellow?"

"Can we not get a message out at least? Warning of some threat?"

"That feels like failure, Watson. Waving a white flag. Only in your case a shirt. I don't want to be reduced to that."

"Have it your way, Holmes."

"I shall." You return to the Stradivarius.

► *Turn to 61.*

THE TRUTH WILL OUT

The correct sequence of notes opens the lock and the door of the cage swings outwards.

"What on earth?" Odon says.

"The lock was made so that it could be opened by the right sequence of notes," you murmur.

"Ah – I didn't know..." he looks deeply puzzled.

"The power of love!" Watson exclaims. "If it's true what they say about Mark Smeaton making the lock for his queen. And those notes, old man, they remind one of the sequence we heard so faintly in the Tower, each time . . . In the end, Holmes, my historical knowledge rather came in useful?"

He is right. Those notes. You all exit the cage and push through the heavy fabric. Outside the concert looks set to start imminently. You, Watson and Odon manage to lose yourselves in the crowd. Rather gleefully, you watch Inspector Lestrade approaching alongside a tall, thin monk you guess must be Andor.

"And I can now reveal that we will find the Crown Jewels here where my brother and his accomplices are imprisoned . . ." He leads them into the folds of fabric surrounding the cage. You all three stride across and hear his words trail away and laughter and jeers ring out.

Coming back out Lestrade is speaking, "The cage is empty – apart from the Jewels. This rather puts you in the frame yourself, my good man. How did you know the Jewels were here?"

"Good morning, Brother Andor," you smile, stepping forward, "Lestrade." You point to Andor: "Here is your villain, Inspector. He has been scheming with our old friend James Moriarty to defraud the historic Pannonhalma Abbey. May I introduce Andor's sibling, the composer Odon von Mihalovic? He is here because he tried to prevent Andor, and so this supposed holy man attempted to frame his own brother as a thief."

"I believe you have some explaining to do, Brother Andor," Lestrade says, taking a firm hold of him. "Please ensure the Jewels are taken to a safe place, Constable Nelson." Lestrade gestures to one of his subordinates.

"Now Odon," you say, "We must get along to the concert. Come along, Watson."

▶ *Turn to 84.*

93 IN THE PULPIT

from 55

"Where are you going, Watson?

"I'm looking for a book," he declares loudly, striding off across the church. "The clue said, *Spelling out in five . . .*"

"What would we do if we found one?" you say rather snappishly.

"Maybe look up the fifth word, or decipher some code," he snaps back.

You look at him rather scornfully. He is twirling his ridiculous moustache. Then he climbs down wearily. "There are no books up there or anywhere I can see in the chapel, anyway."

You're both feeling stumped. What about 'Be sure to flip', you wonder?

▶ *Turn to 71.*

94 A GREEN SHOT

from 67

"It's got to be green!" Watson almost shouts. "See here," he says, lifting the code wheel from your hands. "This 24 is green. The existing score is 76, I do believe, and 76 added to 24 is 100!"

You can't fault dear old Watson's maths, but you do perhaps have a question or two about his logic.

You respond: "We do need to get as close to 100 as we can, but we can't risk going over, and I do believe that by targeting green, that possibility is indeed present."

Watson opens his mouth, then closes it again. The two of you return to the puzzle.

▶ *Return to 67.*

LOCKED IN

"Hello, old chap," Odon says lugubriously, walking slowly over.

"What the devil!" You splutter. "Why didn't you warn us or try to get out when we opened the door?"

"I didn't know who it was coming in. I was keeping well away. And I did try and call out, but the fabric is thick and it must have muffled the message. It's a booby trap, my dear Holmes. We're locked in. As for trying to escape, well, I would be playing into their hands. I decided that the only way out of this is to play the game to the end," he said.

"And win," you say.

"But it looks like I have lost," he says gloomily.

Scattered around the room, poking out of bags, strewn across the floor, are the missing Crown Jewels. A part of you wants to take a moment to marvel at them. An incredible amount of wealth sits with you in this room.

"We know about your plot," Watson says, turning to Odon and sighing, "that you planned to reveal Brother Andor's plans for the monastery at today's concert."

"Indeed," Odon responds, "Brother Andor and Moriarty, I should say. They've been building this plot together for years. Moriarty travelled to Hungary to take refuge at the monastery following your time together at the Reichenbach Falls, and it was there they hatched the plan."

You nod. It's all falling into place.

"Andor tried to recruit me, and I knew I needed to share his disastrous plan with the world, somewhere 'neutral' but high-profile. I had to let them think their plan was working but expose them at the last minute. I believed this concert a good fit for that. They must have found out somehow and have now trapped me here with the Crown Jewels to discredit my name and obscure my message." Odon raises his voice. "No one will trust me after this, Holmes. They will have the monastery. They will have won."

"Trapped us here, not won," you correct him. You consider the room once more and take in your predicament.

▶ *Turn to 40.*

KING'S PRIVATE CHAPEL IN THE WAKEFIELD TOWER

Eager to get on, you lead Watson towards the Wakefield Tower and into a large, central room. You find yourself hurrying.

But once there, you stand perfectly still, casting your eyes about, searching for an indication of where Moriarty's chain of clues could be leading next.

Watson's reading about the Tower is still 'bearing fruit'. You sigh. He leans the violin case against the wall and reads: "They began building the Wakefield Tower in 1220," he says. "Originally the Blundeville Tower. May have changed the name when they used it to lock up prisoners captured in the Battle of Wakefield. Historians believe it was where the king had his apartments."

Information, speculation. You want hard facts that will help you unpick the mystery facing you tonight. You want to remind Watson that you are working against the clock, but for some reason you remain silent.

He is calling you across.

"This is the king's private chapel. King Henry VI may have been murdered – stabbed – here at prayer. On 21 May, 1471. Though some say he died of grief on hearing his son Edward had been killed on the battlefield. They also say his ghost haunts the Tower . . ."

But now you are happy for him to chatter on. You have found your clues in the chapel.

"Great Scott!" he shouts. "Are those words on the wall written in blood?"

"I would put nothing past Moriarty," you say.

▶ *Use the clues in the scene to find a number and turn to that number paragraph.*

We're all looking
for meaning . . .
Combine, Count.

HiNts

aNd

SOLutIoNs

221A - HINTS

(1) 'Sweet Thames Run Softly'
Consider the symmetry of the letters. What might 'shift in the cross' mean in the message? Look closely at the phrase 'Estaablish their position' to work out how to use what you find.

(5) The Jewel Room
What could 'take a step forward' mean if you're thinking about decoding a hidden message?

(6) Dinner in the Salt Tower
There must be a significance in the number of items each diner has? Think laterally for a way to use the number of items to identify your destination. What significance might there be in our only considering the diners' second names.

(11) Lanthorn Tower
Are there matching totals for the pentagons? And is there a connection between the numbers facing directly on matching sides of the pentagons?

(13) In the Shrubbery
It might be worth remembering the bar of music you find here.

(14) A Musical Note
It might be worth remembering the bar of music you find here.

(15) To The Coldharbour Tower
What is normally used to hold wine? If you're stuck, turn to 77 for further clues.

(16) The Cell
What might the words 'consider your position' indicate when thinking in terms of converting numbers to words? Perhaps the final word of the message (before the signature) is meant as a further prompt.

(19) **E**

If every number from 1 to 25 has to appear in the square, what might that mean for the totals of each column, row or diagonal?

(20) **Traitors' Gate**

What is the configuration in which all the statements are true? Which cannonball would you find in the bottom-right position?

(21) **To the Window (Lanthorn Tower)**

What could be the importance of finding your initials written out? How might that give you a clue in decoding the short message?

(22) **In the Crypt**

You are looking for ten symbols altogether. If you haven't yet, take a close look at the alcove.

(24) **Flint Tower**

What do 'L', 'R', 'D' and 'U' probably mean in terms of directional instructions? Work your way backwards by following the opposite of the coded written instruction.

(30) **Well Tunnel**

What is the gap between 'Y' and 'F'?

(35) **Stores**

Some spinning and scrambling wouldn't go amiss.

(40) **MSAB**

How might the bars of music you discovered through the night be useful here?

(41) **First Light**

For 9 across, if you are stuck, look at (listen to) entry 9.

43 **Outside the Waterloo Barracks**
This is about sequential differences. Look at the way the symbols move as the sequence progresses.

44 **White Tower**
Do you notice anything odd about the position of the wind vanes?

48 **Bowyer Tower**
The second word horizontally and vertically should be a familiar one to music lovers. Holmes and Watson took in this form of musical entertainment in Doyle's short story: 'The Adventure of the Red Circle'.

50 **At the Bell Tower Window**
Look at how, and whether, the designs touch one another.

51 **Salt Tower Chimney – A Note**
The phrase *I know you are not fathers but if you were where would you look for your baby?* suggests the word 'cradle' to Holmes.

52 **Strad**
It might be worth remembering the bar of music you find here.

55 **Queens Quiescent**
Think about where you are and what might be below.

56 **Cradle Tower**
What happens if you start at the centre?

58 **St John's Chapel**
The clockface nudges you to view the sequence of pillars in a clockwise direction – that is, left to right. How do the number of the grey bricks change from pillar to pillar? Can you see any pattern behind the growing number of grey bricks?

(60) **The Bloody Tower**
The first letter in the answer is the fourth of the missing letters in the clue.

(63) **Triangulation**
Use the corners.

(66) **Another Tune**
It might be worth remembering the bar of music you find here.

(67) **Headquarters of the Fusiliers**
What might cause a particular colour to tip you over the edge?

(68) **Yeoman Warders' Club**
What's the difference between an empty glass of wine and a full glass, really?

(70) **Tower View**
Try counting? And can you think of an easy way to translate letters into numbers? How many letters are there in the alphabet?

(73) **Follow the Music**
Consider where you are. What is the mirror image of going forwards? If a mirror inverts a direction, what does it do to a number?

(74) **Another String**
It might be worth remembering the bar of music you find here.

(75) **Priceless Gems**
Think carefully about the minimum number needed for all three types of gem.

76 **Devereux Tower Second Storey**
What is the effect of crossing out the three letters in the puzzling word 'Spinum'?

77 **Inspecting the Coldharbour Ruins**
What could 'Take a step back and look closely' mean in terms of using the code wheel?

80 **St Thomas's Tower**
Consider the message.
What happens at the beginning?
Where might that be leading us?
Be sure to look for directions.

88 **Byward Tower**
Perhaps some words in the text are more influential than others. Where do they lead you?

90 **Tower Bridge**
You've noted there are differences between the drawing and the view. How many? What could 'Initially' take note mean? Note also the words 'bring them together'.

96 **King's Private Chapel in the Wakefield Tower**
Combine comes before *count* in the message scrawled on the wall. What element in the scene can be combined and then counted? *We're all looking for meaning?* What does that suggest?

221B - SOLUTIONS

1 'Sweet Thames Run Softly'

The message instructs you to look at the street signs (with the arrows) and identify those that don't 'shift in the cross', indicating letters unchanged by two lines of symmetry. These letters are H, I, O. You're then invited to 'establish their position'; this instruction is asking you to find the number of their place in the alphabet. (There is an additional clue in the emboldening of the letters in the phrase 'Estaablish their position' and the misspelling – the emboldened letters are an anagram of the word 'alphabet'.) The first letters of each sentence in the message spell NUMBER to further illuminate this clue. These numbers are H - 8, I - 9, O - 15. There are 3 Os, 2 Hs and 1 I in the street signs. You bring them together by adding the numbers. 15 + 15 + 15 + 8 + 8 + 9 = 70. Turn to 70.

5 The Jewel Room

The four symbols decode as KKDA. But the clue said you should take a step forward to decode. If you move the wheel one step round you get LLEB. The clue also said turn around, so if you reverse the word order you get BELL. The next destination is the Bell Tower, marked 50 on the map. Turn to 50.

6 Dinner in the Salt Tower

This puzzle demands lateral thinking. The code requires you to count the number of objects each diner has and use the letter of that number in their name to form a word: the next destination. We know they are dining left to right in this order and have been alerted to consider their second names only: Castiglioni – one item, first letter, C; Gerard – three items, third letter, R; Arden – one item, first letter, A; Moody – four items, fourth letter, D; Balliol – three items, third letter, L; Draper – five items, fifth letter, E. The destination is CRADLE. On the map, Cradle Tower, marked 56, is close. The additional clue at 51 indicates you should think of a place where a father would look for his baby. Turn to 56.

(11) Lanthorn Tower

The numbers on each pentagon add up to 50. The numbers on facing sides of neighbouring pentagons, when multiplied, equal 27. The missing numbers are 17, 21, 9, 13, 20, 17, which translate, using the code wheel, to W, I, N, D, O, W. Go to the window. The second number in the sequence is 21. Go to 21.

(15) To the Coldharbour Tower

The riddle indicates you should look for something that can hold wine and could shine in sunlight. Turn to 77 for further confirmation of what it is.

(16) The Cell

The tallied numbers on the wall are 5, 18, 5, 20 and 16. The word 'position' in Moriarty's note is directing you to think of the position of each letter in the alphabet. If A=1, B=2 etc., then the numbers spell E, R, E, T, P – which can be unscrambled to spell PETER, directing you to the Church of St Peter ad Vincula, marked 37 on the map. Turn to 37.

(19) E

The circled number, as shown on the completed square in the graphic, is 15. Look up 15 on the map to find your destination: the Coldharbour Tower.

1	23	16	4	21
15	14	7	18	11
24	17	13	9	2
20	8	19	12	6
5	3	10	22	25

20 **Traitors' Gate**

The T has to be at one end of the bottom row because these are the only places where one ball touches only two others ('T is touching only P and A'). Remember that all the cannonballs must move ('All move'). It must be on the right-hand side because the lower-case letters are on the left ('the leftmost two are not capital'). 'You will i Am sure come out on top' indicates that i and A should be the top two. Therefore T, St Thomas's Tower, is the correct answer. St Thomas's Tower is 80 on the map; turn to 80.

21 **To the Window (Lanthorn Tower)**

The fact that your initials and those of Watson are written in the note indicates that you should take the initial letters of the words in the message to spell out the next destination – 'Sherlock Always Look Twice' – SALT. Turn to the Salt Tower, numbered 6 on the map. We do not know for sure what the H stands for in JHW; the doctor is referred to as John H Watson in Conan Doyle. But some, including the scriptwriters for the BBC TV version of the *Sherlock* stories, claim it stands for Hamish; the BBC show also suggests that Sherlock's full name is William Sherlock Scott Holmes, but the great detective is known only as Sherlock Holmes in Conan Doyle. Turn to 6.

22 **In the Crypt**

The symbol decoding as F is hidden in the large archway. The symbol decoding as L is at the bottom of the ornate stone slab directly ahead. The symbol decoding as I is at the top of the stone slab to the left. The symbol decoding as N is just below the large archway, marked onto the wall. The symbol decoding as T is directly above the ornate stone slab (ahead). The symbol decoding as T is also directly above the smaller stone slab in the left corner. The symbol decoding as O is at the bottom of the ornate stone slab (directly below L). The symbol decoding as W is the shape that surrounds the engraved text within the archway. The symbol decoding as E is directly above this, cut into the wall. The symbol decoding as R is on the stand of the small font on the left. The next location is the Flint Tower. Using the map you will see this is marked as number 24. Turn to 24.

(24) Flint Tower
Answer: see graphic. The next destination is the Lanthorn Tower, numbered 11. Turn to 11.

(30) Well Tunnel
Go left. The message is written in a Caesar shift cipher – named after its reputed originator, the Roman general Julius Caesar. This is a type of code in which the alphabet is imagined as a loop and all the letters shift a set number of places. Here, letters have been moved by 7 places: H becomes A and G becomes Z. When decoded, the message reads: FOR THE THAMES, GO LEFT.

(35) Stores
The numbers can be converted into letters using the code wheel. The numbers 1, 7, 19, 20, 20, 26, 26, 26 reveal the following letters: P, H, E, O, O, T, T, T. Unscrambled, this reads: TO THE TOP, sending you to the attic, marked 32 on the map. Turn to 32.

(40) MSAB
MSAB (Mark Smeaton/Anne Boleyn?) has been threaded through the night, bringing together bars of music and information about the composer Mark Smeaton. You have found four bars of music, each with a one-word title. These bars should be read in the following order: For, My, Sweet, Love. Previously, in passage 19, you heard this as a full phrase, attributed to Smeaton by Watson. The sequence of notes that can be seen on the lock tell you which note to pay attention to in each bar. This, combined with the

letter key in passage 52, indicates that the correct sequence of notes is F, D, G, B. You play these notes, and the lock opens. Turn to 92.

(41) First Light

The completed crossword should look as shown. The ringed letters spell WAKE (a word well-suited to your current condition as you try to shake off sleep) and spell the first part of your next destination Wakefield Tower, numbered 36 on the map. Turn to 36.

(43) Outside the Waterloo Barracks

The answer is as shown in the graphic. The G symbol moves up and down in the left two squares, so should end in the lower left square. The H symbol moves from lower left to upper right and back and so should end in the upper right square. The E symbol moves from lower right to upper left and back and so should end in the upper left square. The Q symbol moves up and down in the right two squares and should end in the lower right square. The two right letters top-down are H and Q, indicating Fusiliers' HQ, marked 67 on the map. Turn to 67.

(44) White Tower

The two wind vanes must have been positioned by hand because neither is pointing in the direction of the breeze. Including the two wind vanes, there are five arrows visible: two facing right (E), one up (N), one down (S), one left (W). When these are put together, there is one loop of arrows that cancels itself out, so you are directed East. This leads you to the Stores, marked 35 on the map. Turn to 35. (Note: "Elementary, my dear Watson" is often quoted as the way Holmes puts down his companion while offering an explanation. In fact, in the Conan Doyle stories Holmes never uses the phrase. He does say "Elementary" – for example, in the 1893 story "The Adventure of the Crooked Man"; "Elementary, my dear Watson," appeared in film scripts not written by Conan Doyle and passed into the parlance of our times.)

48 **Bowyer Tower**
The missing letter is E
R O T A S
O P E R A
T E N E T
A R E P O
S A T O R
Converting E to a number using the code wheel sends you to 19.

50 **At the Bell Tower Window**
Where one of the designs touches an adjacent grid opening, the design in that opening must touch it. The missing piece is A: go to 88.

55 **Queens Quiescent**
The riddle suggests that you should count the number of shields (3). 'Tell' can also mean count, so 'tell the tails' indicates that you count the number of tails on the shields (25). Using the code A=1 . . . Z=26 gives you C for the first and Y for the third. 'Your way below' suggests a destination beneath ground. What five-letter word for an underground destination begins in C and has Y has its third letter? The answer is CRYPT. To find the next paragraph, use the code T=20 minus C=3 = 17. Turn to 17.

56 **Cradle Tower**
68 is the correct answer, as shown in the graphic. You next destination is the Yeoman Warders' Club, marked 68 on the map.

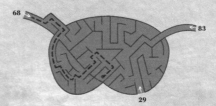

(58) **St John's Chapel**

The answer is 31. Note that the furthest left column has 1 dark grey brick; the second furthest left column has 3 dark grey bricks; the next, 7; the next 13; the second furthest right, 21. How many grey bricks should be on the column furthest to the right, the one covered in paint? To solve this, we need to think about the place of each number in the sequence – sometimes referred to as the 'term'. So we'd think of 1 (pillar 1) being the first term, and 7 (pillar 3) being the third term.

Here, to work out the value of each term:

1. You take the number of that term (i.e. for the first term in the sequence you take 1, for the fourth you take 4).
2. You square that number (you multiply it by itself).
3. You subtract the number of the previous term (i.e. for the first term you subtract 0, for the fourth term you subtract 3).

For example, 1st term: 1x1 - 0 = 1, 4th term: 4x4 - 3 = 13
The missing number is the sixth term of the sequence, so: 6x6 - 5 = 31.
Turn to 31.

(60) **The Bloody Tower**

The full message should read:
'They never knew adulthood
Two royal sons of great promise
Bloodily cut down in their innocence
Did their merciless uncle act heinously?'
The letters e, a, p, b, u, m, c, a, h can be rearranged to form Beauchamp. Go to the Beauchamp Tower, passage 16.

(63) **Triangulation**

There are 25 triangles in total: 9 exist individually and the remaining 16 are made up of these triangles combined, or the triangles combined with other shapes. Looking at the map you can find your next destination: the Well Tower, marked 25. Turn to 25. For the full solution, go to:
https://www.ammonitepress.com/gift/sherlock-tower-of-london-triangles/

67 **Headquarters of the Fusiliers**

The correct answer is Red. If you translate the letters to numbers (F = 3, M = 18, T = 26), looking at the targets that have already been hit, your current total is 76.

The key to this puzzle is using the code wheel to determine the highest possible number connected with each colour (you have no control over which number is added to your score).

The highest possible score you can get with a red target is 22.

The highest possible score you can get with a blue target is 25.

The highest possible score you can get with a green target is 26.

Scores of 25 and 26 would send you over 100 (101 and 102).

Red is the only target that will increase your score with no chance of losing. Proceed to 48, Bowyer Tower.

68 **Yeoman Warders' Club**

The correct answer is 9, as shown in the graphic. If you pick up the second glass, pour the liquid in it into the fifth and then return it to its position you are left with a sequence

42   9   54

of: full glass, empty glass, full glass, empty glass, full glass, empty glass. Turn to 9, Waterloo Barracks on the map.

70 **Tower View**

Looking at the scene, count the number of items in the note. There are 20 railings, 18 windows, 1 boat with a tall mast, 9 barges and 15 trees. Using a simple alphabet code, where 1=A, 2=B . . . 26=Z, convert this to the word 'Traitor'. This suggests 'Traitors' Gate', the traditional way into the Tower through which Princess Elizabeth was taken on Palm Sunday, 1554. Taking the first letter of the word you have made (T), you convert it back to a number (20) using the same conversion method; you turn to 20. You and the good doctor are heading to Traitors' Gate.

(73) Follow the Music

The mirror writing indicates you should do the mirror image of the instructions in the graphic. Instead of going forward as indicated by the forward arrow you should go backwards. And instead of 12 paces forward as the direction shows, you should turn around and go back 21 steps. Go back 21 places from 73 to 52. Turn to 52.

(75) Priceless Gems

Seven. If you pull out six gems, it is still possible to only have two gems of each type: two rubies, two diamonds, two emeralds. However, since the seventh gem needs to be either a ruby, a diamond or an emerald, the seventh gem will bring the total of one type to three, making seven the answer. Looking at the map, the location marked 7 is the Constable Tower. You and Watson are headed there. Turn to paragraph 7.

(76) Devereux Tower Second Storey

The word 'Spinum' indicates two things. First: do not spin the code wheel. Second: delete 'pin' to make the word 'Sum'. This suggests that this is a counting puzzle: what could you count? There must be significance in the letters A, L, written beneath. Count the number of times A and L appear in the message. The answer is 5 and 8. Turn to 58 on the map: St John's Chapel in the White Tower.

(77) Inspecting the Coldharbour Ruins

Use the code wheel to translate the message. 'Take a step back and look closely' indicates you should move back one position to identify the letter. The message spells out: 'Have some bottle'. You decide you need to look for a bottle to find the next clue. The third letter is V, which translates to 2. Turn to 2.

(80) St Thomas's Tower

The correct brick is 23. The solution to this puzzle lies in the cryptic message scratched into the brickwork. The underlined 'begin' points us to the beginning of each line. "What direction are you headed?" suggests that directions are important. Taking the first letter of each line allows us to transform it into a direction: A becomes Above, R becomes Right, B becomes Below, L becomes Left. We then need to connect each of these directions to the image described in that line. We're looking for the brick above the fire, to the right of the moon, below the sun and to the left of the lightning. The only brick that fits all of these directions is 23, the correct answer.

(88) Byward Tower

You should go to Devereux Tower. The emboldened letters in the text invite you to do the following: Start with A. Turn Six Places Left. Starting at A, and turning six places left leaves your code wheel showing the colour green. Green is the colour of the ground in the image. Following the instructions below the mural, you are sent to Devereux. Turn to 45.

(90) Tower Bridge

The answer is 59. First you need to determine which items are missing in the sketch. They are as follows:

1. The flag in the far left of the image
2. A window in the rectangular building in the left of the image.
3. The roof of the building in the far right.
4. The tower in the foreground of the image.
5. The portcullis in the centre of the image.

To solve the puzzle, take the first letter from each missing item: F (flag), W (window), R (roof), T (tower), P (portcullis). Then put these letters into the code wheel to convert them into numbers (3, 17, 12, 26, 1) and then add the numbers together to get their answer: 59. Turn to 59 to continue your adventure.

(96) King's Private Chapel in the Wakefield Tower

Combine the letters to make words. Count the number of words. They have to be words of more than one letter since you are asked to combine. The number of whole words that can be made from the letters C, H, A and T is 5 (Chat, Hat, Cat, Act, At). On the map 5 indicates the upstairs Jewel Room in the Wakefield Tower. Turn to 5.

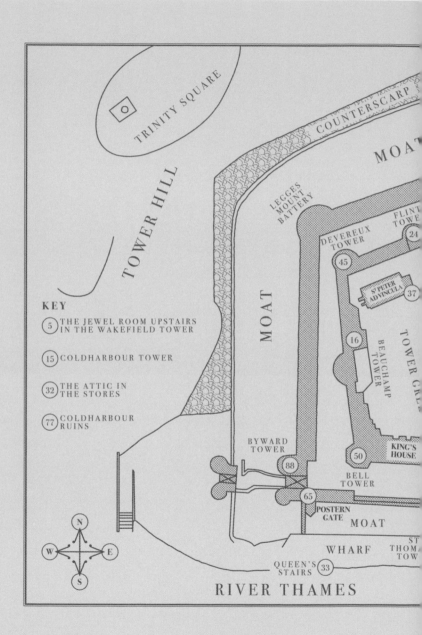

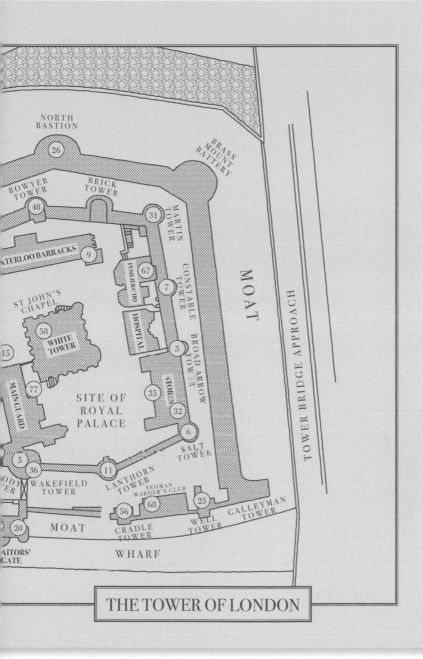

THE TOWER OF LONDON

PLAN OF THE TOWER OF LONDON

First published 2022 by
Ammonite Press
an imprint of Guild of Master Craftsman Publications Ltd
Castle Place, 166 High Street, Lewes, East Sussex, BN7 1XU,
United Kingdom

Reprinted 2023 (twice)

ISBN 978-1-78145-461-9

Publisher: Jonathan Bailey
Design Manager: Robin Shields
Senior Project Editor: Tom Kitch
Editor: Robin Pridy
Consultant: Viv Croot

Colour reproduction by GMC Reprographics
Printed and bound in China

If you've escaped the pages (or are still trapped!) please
send us a message: **#SherlockHolmesEscapeBook**
@ammonitepress

AMMONITE

www.ammonitepress.com